These are
THE SACRAMENTS

These are
THE
SACRAMENTS

as described by Fulton J. SHEEN

as photographed by Yousuf KARSH

HAWTHORN BOOKS, INC.

Publishers • New York

First Printing, November, 1962

Nihil Obstat

WILLIAM F. HOGAN, s.t.d.

CENSOR LIBRORUM

Imprimatur

JAMES A. HUGHES, j.c.d., ll.d., p.a.

VICAR GENERAL, ARCHDIOCESE OF NEWARK

October 22, 1962

CONTENTS

THE SACRAMENTS

A Divine Sense of Humor

No one can ever understand the sacraments unless he has what might be called a "divine sense of humor." A person is said to have a sense of humor if he can "see through" things; one lacks a sense of humor if he cannot "see through" things. No one has ever laughed at a pun who did not see in the one word a twofold meaning. To materialists this world is opaque like a curtain; nothing can be seen through it. A mountain is just a mountain, a sunset just a sunset; but to poets, artists, and saints, the world is transparent like a window pane—it tells of something beyond; for example, a mountain tells of the Power of God, the sunset of His Beauty, and the snowflake of His Purity.

When the Lord Incarnate walked this earth, He brought to it what might be called a "divine sense of humor." There is only one thing that He took seriously, and that was the soul. He said: "What exchange shall a man give for his soul?" Everything else was a tell-tale of something else. Sheep and goats, wine bottles and patches on clothing, camels and eyes of needles, the lightning flash and the red of the sunset sky, the fisherman's nets and Caesar's coin, chalices and rich men's gates—all of these were turned into parables and made to tell the story of the Kingdom of God.

Our Lord had a divine sense of humor, because He revealed that the universe was sacramental. A sacrament, in a very broad sense of the term, combines two elements: one visible, the other invisible—one that can be seen, or tasted, or touched, or heard; the other unseen to the eyes of the flesh. There is, however, some kind of relation or significance between the two. A spoken word is a kind of sacrament, because there is something material or audible about it; there is also something spiritual about it, namely, its meaning. A horse can hear a funny story just as well as a man. It is conceivable that the horse may hear the words better than the man and at the end of the story the man may laugh, but the horse will never give a horse laugh. The reason is that the horse gets only the material side of the "sacrament," namely, the sound; but the man gets the invisible or the spiritual side, namely, the meaning.

A handshake is a kind of sacrament, because there is something seen and felt, namely, the clasping of hands; but there is something mysterious and unseen, namely, the communication of friendship. A kiss is a kind of sacrament: the physical side of it is present if one kisses one's own hand, but the spiritual side of it is missing because there is no sign of affection for another. One of the reasons why a stolen kiss is often resented is that it is not sacramental; it has the carnal side without a spiritual side; that is, the willingness to exchange a mark of esteem or affection.

This book on the sacraments is written because men live in a world that has become entirely too serious. Gold is gold, nuclear warfare is nuclear warfare, dust is dust, money is money. No significance or meaning is seen in the things that make a sound to the ear, or a sight to the eye. In a world without a divine sense of humor, architecture loses decoration and people lose courtesy in their relationships with one another.

When civilization was permeated with a happier philosophy, when things were seen as signs of outward expression of the unseen, architecture was enhanced with a thousand decorations: a pelican feeding her young from her own veins symbolized the sacrifice of Christ; the gargoyle peering from behind a pillar in a cathedral reminded us that temptations are to be found even in the most holy places. Our Lord, on the occasion of His planned entrance into Jerusalem, said that if men withheld their praise of Him, "the very stones would cry out," which they did as, later, they burst into Gothic Cathedrals.

Now the stones are silent, for modern man no longer believes in another world; they have no story to tell, no meaning to convey, no truth to illustrate. When faith in the spiritual is lost, architecture has nothing to symbolize; similarly when men lose the conviction of the immortal soul, there is a decline in the respect for the human. Man without a soul is a thing; something to be used, not something to be reverenced. He becomes "functional" like a building, or a monkey wrench, or a wheel. The courtesies, the amenities, the urbanities, the gentility that one mortal ought to have for another are neglected once man is no longer seen as bearing within himself the Divine Image. Courtesy is not a condescension of a superior to an inferior, or a patronizing interest in another's affairs; it is the homage of the heart to the sacredness of human worth. Courtesy is born of holiness, as ornamentation is born of the sense of the holy. Let us see if ornamentation returns to architecture, if courtesy also returns to human manners; for by one and the same stroke, men will have lost their dull seriousness, and will begin to live in a sacramental universe with a divine sense of humor.

Life is a vertical dimension expressed in the soaring spire, or in the leaping fountain, both of which suggest that earth, history, and nature must be left behind to seek union with the Eternal. Opposite to this is an

8

error which substitutes the horizontal for the vertical, the prostrate form of death for the upright stature of life. It is the disease of secularity and of naturalism. It insists on the ultimacy of the seen and the temporal, and the meaninglessness of the spiritual and the invisible.

Two errors can mar our understanding of the natural world: one is to cut off entirely from Almighty God; the other is to confound it substantially with Him. In the first instance, we have the clock without the clock maker, the painting without the artist, the verse without the poet. In the second instance, we have the forger and the forged rolled into one, the melting and the fusing of the murderer and the victim, the boiling of the cook and his dinner. Atheism cuts off creation from its Creator; pantheism identifies nature with God. The true notion is that the material universe is a sign or an indication of what God is. We look at the purity of the snowflake and we see something of the goodness of God. The world is full of poetry; it is sin which turns it into prose.

The Bible Is A Sacramental

Coming closer to the meaning of sacrament, the Bible is a sacramental in the sense that it has a foreground and a background. In the foreground are the actors, the cult, the temple, the wars, the sufferings, and the glories of men. In the background, however, is the all-pervading presence of God as the Chief Actor, Who subjects nations to judgment according to their obedience or disobedience to the moral law, and Who uses incidents or historical facts as types, or symbols, of something else that will happen. For example, take the brazen serpent in the desert. When the Jewish people were bitten by poisonous serpents, God commanded Moses to make a brazen serpent, and to hang it over the crotch of a tree; all who would look upon that serpent of brass would be healed of the serpent's sting. This apparently was a rather ridiculous remedy for poison and not everyone looked on it. If one could divine or guess their reason, it would probably be because they concentrated on only one side of the symbol; namely, the lifeless, shiny, brass thing hanging on a tree. But it proved to be a symbol of faith: God used that material thing as a symbol of trust or faith in Him.

The symbolism goes still further. The Old Testament is fulfilled in Christ, Who reveals the full mystery of the brazen serpent. Our Lord told Nicodemus that the brass serpent was lifted up in the desert, so that He would have to be lifted up on a Cross. The meaning now became clear: the brass serpent in the desert *looked* like the serpent that bit the people; but though it *seemed* to be the same, it was actually *without* any poison. Our Blessed Lord now says that He is like that brazen serpent. He, too,

9

would be lifted up on the crotch of a tree, a Cross. He would look as if He Himself was filled with the poison of sin, for His Body would bear the marks, and the stings, and the piercing of sin; and yet as the brass serpent was without poison so He would be without sin. As those who looked upon that brass serpent in the desert in faith were healed of the bite of the serpent, so all who would look upon Him on His Cross bearing the sins and poisons of the world would also be healed of the poison of the serpent, Satan.

The word "sacrament" in Greek means "mystery," and Christ has been called by St. Paul "the mystery hidden from the ages." In Him is something divine, something human; something eternal, something temporal; something invisible, something visible. The mystery of Bethlehem was the Son of God taking upon Himself a human nature to unite human nature and divine nature in one Person. He Who, in the language of Scripture, could stop the turning about of the Arcturus, had the prophecy of His birthplace determined, however unconsciously, by a Caesar ordering an imperial census. He Who clothed the fields with grass, Himself was clothed with swaddling bands. He from Whose hands came planets and worlds had tiny arms that were not quite long enough to touch the huge heads of the cattle. He Who trod the everlasting hills was too weak to walk. The Eternal Word was dumb. The Bird that built the nest of the world was hatched therein.

The human nature of Our Blessed Lord had no power to sanctify of and by itself; that is to say, apart from its union with divinity. But because of that union, the humanity of Christ became the efficient cause of our justification and sanctification and will be until the end of the world. Herein is hidden a hint of the sacraments. The humanity of Christ was the bearer of divine life and the means of making men holy; the sacraments were also to become the effective signs of the sanctification purchased by His death. As Our Blessed Lord was the sensible sign of God, so the sacraments were to become the sensible signs of the grace which Our Lord had won for us.

If men were angels or pure spirits, there would have been no need of Christ using human natures or material things for the communication of the divine; but because man is composed of matter and spirit, body and soul, man functions best when he sees the material as the revealer of the spiritual. From the very beginning of man's life, his mother's fondling is not merely to leave an impress upon his infant body, but rather to communicate the sublimely beautiful and invisible love of the mother. It is not the material thing which a man values, but rather what is *signified* by the material thing. As Thomas a Kempis said, "regard not so much the gift of the lover as the love of the giver." We tear price tags from gifts so that there will be no material relationship existing between the love that gave the thing and the

10

thing itself. If man had no soul or spiritual destiny, then communism would satisfy. If man were only a biological organism, then he would be content to eat and to sleep and to die like a cow.

What the Sacraments Bring to Man

The sacraments bring divine life or grace. Christ's reason for taking upon Himself a human nature was to pay for sin by death on the cross and to bring us a higher life: "I have come so that they may have life, and have it more abundantly" (JOHN 10:10). But, it may be said, that man already has life. Indeed he does; he has a biological, physiological life. He once had a higher divine life which he lost. Christ came to bring that life back to man. This higher life which is divine, distinct from the human, is called grace, because it is *gratis* or a free gift of God.

Two tadpoles at the bottom of a pond were one day discussing the problem of existence. One said to the other, "I think I will stick my head out to see if there is anything else in the world." The other tadpole said, "Don't be silly, do you think there is anything else in this world besides water?" So those who live the natural life ignore the beauty of the higher life of grace.

Man may live at three different levels: the sensate, the intellectual, and the divine. These may be likened to a three-story house. The *sensate* level, or the first floor, represents those who deny any other reality except the pleasures that come from the flesh. Their house is rather poorly furnished and is capable of giving intermittent thrills which quickly dry up. The occupant of this first floor is not interested in being told of higher levels of existence; in fact, he may even deny their existence.

On the second floor, there is the *intellectual* level of existence, that of the scientist, the historian, the journalist, the humanist; the man who has brought to a peak all of the powers of human reason and human will. This is a much more comfortable kind of existence, and far more satisfying to the human spirit. Those on the second floor may think their floor is "a closed universe," regarding as superstitious those who desire a higher form of life.

But there is actually a third floor which is the floor of *grace* by which the human heart is illumined by truths which reason cannot know; by which the will is strengthened by a power quite beyond all psychological aids, and the heart is entranced with the love which never fails; which gives a peace that cannot be found on the two lower levels.

There is light outside the window, but it is up to man to open the blinds. The opening of the blinds does not constitute light; it is rather the condition of its entrance. When God made us, He gave us *ourselves*. When He gives

11

us grace, He gives us *Himself*. When He created us, He gave Himself to us in a way which makes us one with Him.

One often sees signs painted on roadways, "Jesus Saves." Now this indeed is true, but the important question is how does He save? What relation have we in the twentieth century to Christ in the first? Do we establish contact with Him only by reading about Him? If that be all, our relationship is not much closer than that which we can have with Plato. If Christ is only a memory of someone who lived centuries ago, then it is rather difficult to see that His influence will be any different than that of Socrates or Buddha.

The answer to the question of how Christ saves is to be found in the sacraments. The divine life of Christ is communicated through His Church or His Mystical Body in exactly the same way that His divine life was communicated when He walked on earth. As He then used His human nature as the instrument of divinity, and used material things as signs and symbols of the conferring of His pardon, so He now uses other human natures and material things as the instruments for the communication of that same divine life.

In the earthly life of Our Lord, we read that there were two kinds of contact. There was the *visible* contact with humanity by which His power was communicated to the palsied man and to the blind, both of whom He touched. But there was also the *invisible* contact, in which Our Blessed Lord showed His power by working miracles at a distance, such as the curing of the servant of the centurion of Nazareth. The second kind of contact is an anticipation of the way that Christ, Who is now in heaven, extends and communicates His power through the sacraments.

Seven Conditions of Life

The physical or the natural life requires seven conditions, five of which refer to the person as an individual, and the other two as a member of society. The five conditions of leading an individual life are: (1) In order to live, one must obviously be born; (2) He must nourish himself, for he who does not eat shall not live; (3) He must grow to maturity, throwing away the things of the child, and assume the responsibilities of adult life; (4) In case he is wounded, he must have his wounds bound and healed; and (5) In case he has disease (for a disease is very different from a wound), the traces of the disease must be driven out. As a member of society two further conditions are required: (1) He must live under government and justice in human relationships, and (2) He is called to propagate the human species.

Over and above this human life, there is the divine Christ-life. The seven conditions of leading a personal Christ-life are the following: (1) We must be spiritually born to it, and that is the Sacrament of Baptism; (2) We must nourish the divine life in the soul, which is the Eucharist; (3) We must grow to spiritual maturity and assume full responsibilities as members of the spiritual army of the Church, which is Confirmation; (4) We must heal the wounds of sin, which is Penance; (5) We must drive out the traces of the diseases of sin, which is the Anointing of the Sick; (6) We must live under the spiritual government of the Church, which is Holy Orders; (7) We must prolong and propagate the Kingdom of God on earth, which is Matrimony.

Every sacrament has an outward or visible sign; for example, in Baptism it is water, in the Eucharist it is bread and wine. But the sacrament also has a *form* or *formula,* or words of spiritual significance given to the *matter* when it is conferred. Three things then are absolutely required for a sacrament: (1) Its institution by Christ; (2) An outward sign; and (3) The power of conferring the grace or divine life purchased for us by the Passion, Death, and Resurrection of Christ.

The Power and Efficacy of the Sacraments

The sacraments derive their power and efficacy from the Passion, Death, and Resurrection of Our Lord. Why was a blood sacrifice required to bring us the seven-fold sanctification? For several reasons: Life is in the blood, but so also is sin. The sins of the alcoholic, the libertine, and the pervert are often written on their faces; their excesses are recorded in every cell of their body and every drop of their blood. If, therefore, sin is to be done away with, there should be some shedding of blood, as if to symbolize the emptying of sin. It is often the death of soldiers that brings freedom to a nation; it is the giving of one's blood to another which heals him of anemia. The blood bank from which others may draw healing is hint of another blood bank from which souls may be healed of the ravages of sin.

Furthermore, blood is the best symbol of sacrifice, because blood is the life of man: when man gives up his blood, he gives up his life. Hence, St. Peter writes:

> What was the ransom that freed you from the vain observances
> of ancestral tradition? You know well enough that it was not paid
> in earthly currency, silver or gold; it was paid in the precious
> Blood of Christ; no lamb was ever so pure, so spotless a victim.
>
> (I PETER 1:18, 19)

The blood of Christ had infinite value because He is a divine person. The life of a lamb is more precious than that of a fly, and the life of a man is more precious than the life of a beast, and the life of the God-Man is more precious than the life of any human being.

Our mind, our will and our conscience become completely sanctified through the application of the merits of Christ:

> "Shall not the Blood of Christ, Who offered Himself, through the Holy Spirit, as a Victim unblemished in God's sight, purify our consciences, and set them free from lifeless observances, to serve the Living God?" (HEB. 9:14)

The Application to the Sacraments

Calvary is like a reservoir of divine life or grace. From it, there flow seven different kinds of sanctification for man in different stages of his spiritual existence. Each of these seven channels is a sacrament by which the power of the Risen Christ is bestowed on souls by a spiritual and effective contact. This divine life pours into the soul when we receive the sacraments, unless we put an obstacle in the way, just as water will not flow out of a faucet if we put our hand in front of the faucet. But a faucet in a house has no power to quench thirst unless there is a reservoir and a pipeline. So the sacraments do not confer grace as magical signs; they communicate it only because they are in contact with the Risen Christ.

What makes the difference between the sacraments is how each is applied to us. The Christ-life affects us in a different way when we are born than when we are about to die; in a different way when we reach the age of responsibility than when we enter into marriage; in a different way when we wound ourselves than when we exercise government. The sunlight is the same whether it shines on mud to harden it or on wax to soften it. It shines on some flowers and makes them grow; it shines on a wound and heals it. So too, the blood of Christ applied at different moments of life results in a different kind of power.

A principle of philosophy states: "Whatever is received is received according to the mode of the one receiving it." If you pour water into a blue glass, it looks blue; if you pour it into a red glass, it looks red. If you pour water into the parched earth, it is quite different than water poured onto a carpet or into oil. So too, when the blood of Christ and its merits flood in upon the soul, it depends upon the one receiving it. Does the soul come for strengthening? For nourishment? For healing? For a long journey? For induction into the spiritual army? The effects will differ as to whether a person is spiritually dead or spiritually living. If a member of the Church is spiritually dead, then it will revive him as does the Sacrament of Penance, or the Sacrament of Baptism.

14

I

THE SACRAMENT
OF BAPTISM

The sunshine, the carbons, and the rain could never share the life of the plant unless they died to their lower existence and were assumed or taken up into plant life. Plants could never share the sensitive and locomotive power of animals, unless they died to their lower existence and were taken up by the animal. None of the things in lower creation could live in man, and share his arts, his sciences, his thinking and his loves unless they ceased to be what they were, submitting to the death of knife and fire.

Now, since there is a life above the human, the Christ-life, man, or the old Adam, cannot share in it unless he dies to himself. But here there is no confiscation or violent appropriation as there is when the cow eats grass. Christ will not take us up to Himself unless we freely give ourselves to Him. This death to the life of sin, this sharing of the divine life, is Baptism.

Water: The Material Sign of Baptism

Water is used for cleansing from dust and dirt; therefore, it may be the symbol of a *spiritual washing* from original sin. But it can also symbolize both death and life. One can plunge into water and be submerged by it; then it is a symbol of *death*. After the plunge, one may rise from the water; then it is a token of *resurrection*. A descent into water has always been a description of penetration into deep and mysterious fecundities; the Greeks believed that the whole living universe came from water.

From another point of view, water is an excellent symbol of Baptism, because it is an open sign of *separation*. Water very often is the natural

15

boundary between city and city, state and state, nation and nation, continent and continent, tribe and tribe. Those who live on one side of water are "separated" from those who live on the other. In the early days, before rapid communication, it was a dramatic experience to pass from one territory to another. This symbolism, therefore, was well fitted for the Divine Master to indicate the separation of the Christian from the world, as the water which was divided in the Red Sea, was a symbol of the separation of Israel from the slavery of Egypt.

Once the Jews had crossed the Red Sea, another symbol was used to "separate" them as the people of God, and that was circumcision. Not only was it a token of their covenant or testament with God, but it was required of all Israelites who partook of the Passover. In the New Testament, the same order is followed. Baptism, or incorporation into the Church, is the condition of reception of the New Passover, the Eucharist.

As ranchers brand their cattle, as ancient Romans branded their slaves, so God branded His own, both in the Old Testament and in the New; with circumcision of the flesh in the Old and circumcision of the spirit, or Baptism, in the New.

It may be objected, what good does a little water do when poured upon the head of a child? One might just as well ask what does a little water do when poured into the boiler. The water in the boiler can do nothing of and by itself, nor can the water on the head of a child. But when the water in the boiler is united to the mind of an engineer, it can drive an engine across a continent or a ship across the sea. So too, when water is united to the power of God, it can do more than change a crystal into life. It can take a creature and convert him into a child of God.

Naaman in the Old Testament was something like those today who think of the power of Baptism coming from water rather than from the Passion of Christ. Naaman was the general of the king of Syria. A maid who came from Samaria said that she wished that he had known the great prophet of Israel, for he could have cured him. The king then bade Naaman to go to Israel where he met the prophet, Eliseus. Eliseus said to him: "Go and wash seven times in the Jordan, and thy flesh shalt recover health and thou shalt be clean." Naaman was insulted because he was told to go to that insignificant river Jordan to bathe:

> 'Why', he said angrily, 'I thought he would come out to meet
> me, and stand here invoking the name of his God; that he would
> touch the sore with his hand and cure me. Has not Damascus its
> rivers, Abana and Pharphar, such water as is not found in Israel?'
>
> (IV KINGS 5:11, 12)

16

His servants, however, bade him go wash and be made clean, and he went down and washed seven times according to the word of the man of God, and his flesh was restored and was made like the flesh of a little child when he was made clean. Then he confessed that it was done by the power of God: "I have learned, he said, past doubt, that there is no God to be found in all the world, save here in Israel" (IV KINGS 5:15).

Baptism and the Life of Christ

Under the Old Law people believed in, or yearned for, a Messias who was to come. Abraham believed and his faith was accounted to him as justice, and he received circumcision as a sign of faith.

What was the faith, therefore, that justified Abraham, who was the father of the Jews? It was the faith in the Messias, or the Christ Who was to come. There is no salutary faith except in Christ. The Jews believed in the Christ Who *was to come;* we believe in Christ Who *has come.* The times have changed, but the reality of faith has not changed. There is only one faith. The faith that saves all men, making them pass from carnal generation to spiritual birth.

The reason Our Lord was baptized was because it was part of the whole process of emptying, of humiliation, of the Incarnation. How could He be poor with us, if He did not in some way conform to our poverty? How could He come among sinful men to redeem them, if He did not also reveal the necessity of being purged from sin? There was no need of Our Blessed Mother to submit to the rite of purification, as there was no need of Our Lord to submit to the rite of Baptism by John. He had no need personally of having sins remitted, but He assumed a nature which was related to sinful humanity. Though He was without sin, He appeared to all men as a sinner, as He did on the cross. That was why He walked into the Jordan with all the rest of the sinners to demand the baptism of penance "in remission of sins."

In a very special way, Baptism is related to the death and Resurrection of Christ. In order to be saved, we have to recapitulate in our own lives the Death and the Resurrection of Christ. What He went through, we have to go through. He is the pattern, and we have to be modeled after Him. He is the die, we are the coins that have to be stamped with His image. In all of the sacraments, the virtue of the Passion and Resurrection of Christ is in some way applied to us. In Baptism, there is a very close relationship between the burial and the resurrection. The catechumen is plunged into the water as Christ was plunged into death. We say plunged into death because of the words of Our Lord: "There is a baptism I must needs be baptized with, and how impatient am I for its accomplishment" (LUKE 12:50). Baptism not only incorporates us to the death of that which is evil in us, but also to the Resurrection of Christ, and therefore, to a new life.

There was recently found an inscription on a baptistry erected in the time of Constantine in the beginning of the fourth century, and it reads: "The waters received an old man, but brought forth a new man." St. Paul speaks of this: "It follows, in fact, that when a man becomes a new creature in Christ, his old life has disappeared, everything has become new about him" (II CORINTH. 5:17).

The Blessing of Baptismal Water

The water used in Baptism is blessed on Holy Saturday after the Litany of Saints, whose intercession is invoked on all those who will receive the sacrament. Then follows a prayer asking God to send forth "the Spirit of adoption" on those who are to be baptized. God has one Son Who exhausts the fullness of His glory, but baptism gives Him millions of adopted sons because it makes them partakers of His divine nature. The baptismal water is blessed by a prayer which recalls beautifully all the events of salvation which were in any way connected with water, from the beginning of the world when God's Spirit hovered over the water, down to the commandment of Christ to baptize.

Throughout the Old Testament water is represented as a sinister element, and is supposed to be the abode of demons. To confirm this idea, the *Apocalypse* affirms that there will be no sea in the new earth after the resurrection of the just. Water, because of its unholy association, is exorcised on Holy Saturday that it may become "holy and innocent." The priest then takes the water, divides it into four quarters of the globe to symbolize the four waters that branched out of Paradise and covered the earth. Next, he breathes upon the water three times symbolizing the Holy Spirit, then dips the paschal candle (the symbol of the risen Christ) into it three times. Here the consecration formula uses the symbolism of human generation: "May the power of the Holy Spirit descend into this brimming font, and make the whole substance of this water fruitful in regenerative power." And again, "Just as the Holy Spirit came down upon Mary and wrought in her the birth of Christ, so may He descend upon the Church, and bring about in her maternal womb (the font), the rebirth of God's children."

18

The baptismal font in a church is now generally placed as far from the altar as possible. It often is a corner to the left of the entrance. In the early Church, the baptistry was sometimes placed outside the Church. The reason is that the person about to be baptized was not yet a member of the Church and, therefore, was not allowed to participate in its mysteries.

The baptismal font, if properly erected, has steps going down into it, to indicate that it is a pool. Its shape was octagonal, because the Resurrection took place on the eighth day, or the day after the Jewish Sabbath.

In the Old Testament, circumcision was always performed on the eighth day. The son that David had through his sin with Bethsabee died on the seventh day. The first seven days were symbols of the bonds of sin; hence, the eighth day represented the breaking of those bonds and the liberation from them. In the New Testament, Easter is the eighth day *par excellence*, and that was the reason why Baptism was administered on Easter.

Baptism in the Early Church

Baptism was usually given the night before Easter Sunday, but the baptismal ceremonies began with the opening of Lent. At that time all of the candidates, converts, or catechumens had their names inscribed by a priest in the Church. They were then brought before a bishop who examined the candidates concerning their moral life. Generally, the bishop would bring out the fact that the candidate for Baptism had lived under Satan, but now he must abandon him. This meant a conflict and a battle. That is why we still have in the Church the Gospel of the temptation of Christ for the first Sunday of Lent, because it was the theme of the bishop to the catechumens at the beginning of their instructions.

The ceremony of Baptism took place then in three places and in like manner today: (1) Before the entrance to the Church, which in the early Church was at the beginning of Lent; (2) Inside the Church and before one comes to the baptistry, which happened in the middle of Lent in the early Church; and (3) Finally, the baptistry itself on Holy Saturday night, or Easter morning.

In the baptismal ritual, the stole of the priest at the beginning of the Baptism is violet in color; this is because in the early Church, the first part of the ceremony of Baptism was during Lent. Toward the end of the ceremony, the priest changes his stole to white, following again the tradition of the early Church, when Baptism was administered on Easter Sunday.

20

Outside the Church

The Dialogue

The Baptism begins with a dialogue. The ceremony begins with: "What do you ask of the Church of God?" The answer is: "Faith." The priest asks: "What does faith offer you?" The candidate or his sponsors answer: "Eternal life." Note the close connection between faith and Baptism. After His Resurrection, Our Lord said to His Apostles: "Go out all over the world and preach the gospel to the whole of creation; he who believes and is baptized will be saved; he who refuses belief will be condemned" (MARK 16:15, 16).

Our Blessed Lord first put belief before being baptized. In order to be saved, one must believe *and* be baptized. One can be saved by faith without the sacramental sign of baptism; that is, through desire or by martyrdom, but he who refuses to believe will be condemned: "For the man who believes in him, there is no rejection; the man who does not believe is already rejected; he has not found faith in the name of God's only-begotten Son" (JOHN 3:18).

The dialogue begins with "What do you ask of the Church of God?" Why the Church? Because the Church precedes the individual, not the individual the Church. When a person is baptized, he is not to be thought of as another brick that is added to an edifice, but rather as another cell united to the Christ-life. The Church expands from the inside out, not from the outside in. The foundation cell of the Church is Christ, and through Baptism, there is a multiplication of the cells of His body until there is a differentiation of functions and the building up of the whole Church. As a child is formed in the womb of the mother, so the Church, as a spiritual mother, forms and gives birth to the children of God. The Christian life resulting from Baptism is not an individual and solitary experience. It is a life in the Church and by the Church. As St. Paul expresses it: "Through faith in Christ Jesus you are all now God's sons" (I CORINTH. 12:4).

Baptism does not first of all establish an individual relationship with Christ, and then accidentally make one a member of His body, the Church. It is the other way around. The baptized person is *first* made a member of the Church, and thus he is incorporated into Christ. Baptism is social by nature. We are made members of Christ's body before being established in our individual relationship with Christ:

> We, too, all of us have been baptized into a single body by the power of a single Spirit, Jews and Greeks, slaves and free men alike; we have all been given drink at a single source, the one Spirit.
> (I CORINTH. 12:13)

21

Sponsors

In Baptism, infants are incorporated into Christ, not through an act of their own will, but through an act of the sponsor who represents the Church and assumes responsibility for the spiritual education of the infant. The parents, of course, must consent to the baptism; the Church refuses to baptize anyone against his or her will, or even to baptize an infant unless there is some guarantee that the child will be raised in the faith. The sponsors are representatives of the Church, not representatives of the parents. They witness the incorporation of the infant into the fellowship of Christ.

It may be asked why should a child be baptized when he has nothing to say about it? Well, why should a child be fed? Is he asked his advice before he is given the family name? If he receives the name of the family, the fortune of the family, the rank of the family, the inheritance of the family, why should he not also receive the religion of the family? In our own country we do not wait until children are twenty-one and then allow them to decide whether or not they want to become American citizens, or whether they want to speak the English language. They are born Americans; so we in Baptism are born members of the Mystical Body of Christ. If one waits until he is twenty-one before learning something about his relation to the Lord Who redeemed him, he will have already learned another catechism, the catechism of his passions, his concupiscences, and his lusts.

Exorcisms

Though the Hebrews had passed through the Red Sea, they were, nevertheless, followed by the Egyptians; so too, though a person is baptized, he is still followed by Satan throughout his life. That is why the baptized person is asked to renounce Satan and all of his seductions. This renouncing of Satan has as its parallel the attachment to Christ or the transfer from one master to another. In Baptism today, the ceremonies of exorcism follow rapidly upon one another, and thereby have lost the significance which they had in the early Church when they were separated by several weeks. This evil that the baptized are invited to combat, is not just a moral force or a vague kind of paganism; it is a cosmic reality, for the devil is, as Our Lord said, the prince of this world. That is why even before the Church begins the baptism of a person, it blesses water, oil, and salt, in some instances even with exorcisms, in order to snatch them out of the power of Satan.

There is a triple renouncing of Satan which corresponds to the threefold profession of faith:

Question: Do you renounce Satan?
    Answer: I do renounce him.
Question: And all his works?
    Answer: I do renounce them.
Question: And all his allurements?
    Answer: I do renounce them.

This question has reference to the words of St. Paul to the Romans: "Let us abandon the ways of darkness, and put on the armor of light" (ROM. 13:12).

Thus the triple profession of faith accompanies the triple renouncing of Satan, and is bound to a gesture; namely, the anointing with the oil of catechumens. The one who baptizes dips his thumb in oil, and then traces a cross on the breast and between the shoulders of the one to be baptized. Formerly the oil was rubbed all over the body. This was also done on athletes who were engaging in some sport in the arena, but here the signification is spiritual, for it is the beginning of a spiritual competition (I CORINTH. 9:24–27).

The exorcisms look both to the future, as well as to the past, to remind the catechumen that the struggle against the forces of Satan is a confrontation of God and the devil, the devil seeking to dispute the souls which Our Lord won, as he tempted Our Lord in the desert.

In the early Church, the renouncing of Satan was done facing the west. This is because the west is where the light of the sun disappears; therefore, it was regarded even by the ancient Greeks as the place of the gates of Hades; also, because Christ on the Last Day said He would come from the east to the west: "When the Son of Man comes, it will be like the lightning that springs up from the east and flashes across to the west" (MATT. 24:27). The baptismal liturgy of Milan reads: "Ye were turned to the east for he who renounced the demon turns himself to Christ. He sees Him face to face."

In the exorcism, the priest says: "I exorcise you, unclean spirit, in the name of the Father, of the Son, and of the Holy Spirit. Come forth, from this servant of God [name] for He commands you, spirit accursed and damned, He Who walked upon the sea and extended His right hand to Peter as he was sinking. Therefore, cursed devil, acknowledge your condemnation and pay homage to the true and living God; pay homage to Jesus Christ, His Son, and to the Holy Spirit, and depart from the servant

24

of God [name], for Jesus Christ, Our Lord and our God, has called him [her] to His holy grace and blessing, and to the font of Baptism."

When the priest signs the forehead with his thumb in the form of a cross, he says: "Then never dare, cursed devil, to violate the sign of the cross which we are making upon his [her] forehead through Christ Our Lord."

The various exorcisms, the laying on of hands, breathings, and sign of the cross are done in the vestibule of the Church. The second act of the ceremonies takes place at the entrance of the baptistry. The evil spirit has no authority in the holy place; that is why the final exorcism of the devil is at the entrance.

The Body in Baptism

Because the body is to become by Baptism the temple of God, because God dwells in it, it is fitting that it have an important role in the sacrament. Each of the senses are spiritualized in the sacraments: hearing, taste, touch, smell, and sight.

The ears of the baptized person are touched with the words, "Be thou opened." The Hebrew word Our Lord used in opening the ears of the deaf man was *Ephpheta*. The assumption is that the person up to this moment has been deaf to the hearing of the word of God. Now his ears are opened, so that he can understand the word of God, and the confidences which God exchanges with him about the Kingdom of Heaven.

Tasting is testing. Before food goes into the stomach, it passes through the laboratory of the mouth for either approval or disapproval. In the spiritual order, the taste is not for body-food, but soul-food; the material element here used as a symbol for tasting Divine Wisdom and the Eucharist is salt. Placing salt on the tongue of the candidate for Baptism, the Church says: "Satisfy him [her] with the Bread of Heaven that he [she] may be forever fervent in spirit, joyful in hope, zealous in your service." Scripture bids us: "How gracious the Lord is. Taste and prove it" (PSA. 33:9).

The symbolism is that the truths of faith infused at Baptism will be preserved from error; that the person may reflect the savor of Christ in his life, and this taste of salt may be converted into a yearning for the Bread of Life, the Eucharist, which is the end of all the sacraments. When the faith is gone, everything is gone, as Our Lord warned:

> You are the salt of the earth; if salt loses its taste, what is there left to give taste to it? There is no more to be done with it, but throw it out of doors for men to tread it under foot.
>
> (MATT. 5:13)

25

The body, during the ceremony, is touched in three places with oil: on the breast, between the shoulders, and on the head. The first two anointings are with the oil of catechumens, the last with chrism. The sign of the cross is made on the breast with oil to indicate that the heart must love God; between the shoulders to remind us that we are to carry the Cross of Christ; on the head, as a sign of eternal election in Christ Our Lord.

The *Apocalypse,* describing the end of the world, says the destroying angel was "to attack men, such as did not bear God's mark on their foreheads" (APOC. 9:4). The elect will be known, because they have already been signed and have lived up to all the Cross commits them to in this life.

The last anointing with chrism, which takes place after Baptism, is the symbol of the Holy Spirit. In the Old Testament, oil was poured upon the head of the priest (Ex. 29:7), and upon kings (I KINGS 10:1), to render them holy unto the Lord. Pulled out of the powers of darkness by Baptism, the Christian is now transported into the light of God and into His kingdom; that is why he becomes royal. St. Leo bade the faithful: "Recognize, O Christian, thy dignity."

We associate goodness with sweet odors and badness with foul odors. We have a "nose" for detecting the healthy and the unhealthy. This sense of smell is spiritualized in Baptism, and is made to symbolize sanctity or holiness.

The Church speaks of saints as dying in "the odor of sanctity." Sometimes their bodies after death give forth a sweet odor. The saintly Curé of Ars would walk along a line of several hundred persons waiting to go to confession. He would pick out one here and there and put them first in line. When asked how he could do it, he answered: "I can smell sin." As the Church signs the nostrils of the catechumen, she says: "I sign you on the nostrils that you may perceive the sweet fragrance of Christ."

The eyes of the candidate are anointed, as the Church says: "I sign you on the eyes that you may see God's glory." By this is symbolized a new kind of vision: the things of God in addition to the things of earth: "Fix (your) eyes on what is unseen, not on what we can see. What we can see lasts but for a moment; what is unseen is eternal" (II CORINTH. 4:18). Our Blessed Lord spoke of some who had eyes and yet were blind, because they had no faith: "Have you eyes that cannot see?" (MARK 8:18).

As a further example of the role of vision, a lighted candle is given to the one baptized. He is bidden to receive this burning light, and keep the grace of his baptism without blame. This refers to the words of Our Lord: "Your light must shine so brightly before men that they can see your good works, and glorify your Father Who is in Heaven" (MATT 5:16).

26

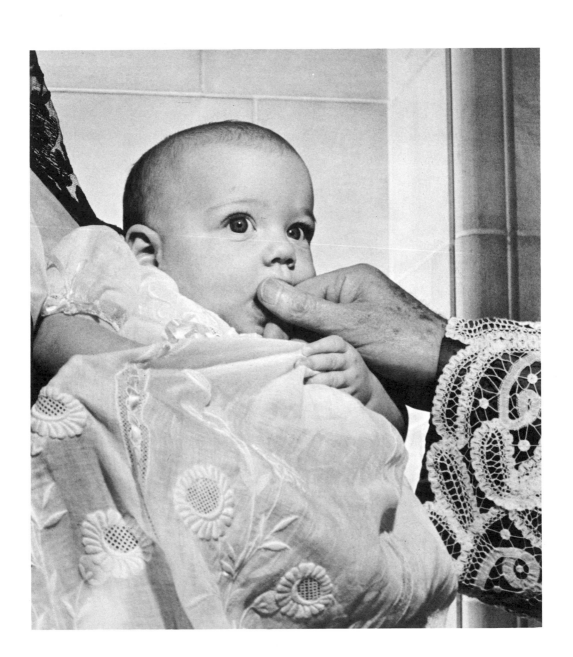

We have the same eyes at night as during the daytime, but we cannot see at night because we lack the light of the sun. So there is a difference in persons looking upon the same reality, such as life, birth, death, the world. The baptized person has a light which the others do not have. Sometimes the person with the light of faith will regard the other person as ignorant or stupid, but actually he is only blind. On the other hand, the one who is baptized must not believe that his superior insights are due to his own reason, or his own merits. They are solely due to the light that has come to him through Christ.

There are various lights in the world: the light of the sun which illumines our senses; the light of reason which illumines science and culture; and the light of faith which illumines Christ and eternal verities.

The Baptism Itself

The actual moment of Baptism comes when the priest pours water on the head of a person, saying: "I baptize thee, in the name of the Father, the Son, and the Holy Spirit." The personal pronoun "I" refers not only to the priest, but to Christ Who speaks through the tongue given Him by the Church as He spoke through the tongue given Him by Mary. As the portals of the flesh once opened to the life of the human, now the womb of the Church opens and exults: "A child is born."

St. Augustine said this is a greater act than the creation of the world, for it blots out our debt of sin to God, original sin if it be an infant, original and personal sins if it be an adult. The full effects of this act will be mentioned later.

The Lighted Candle and Baptism

Because the Sacrament of Baptism opened the eyes of the soul to see, it was called the sacrament of illumination: "Remember those early days, when the light first came to you" (HEB. 10:32). Once asleep to the wonders of Redemption, eyes are now awake to receive Christ, the light of the world (JOHN 1:19) and to become sons of light (I THESS. 5:5).

Because Baptism is the sacrament of faith, it is the sacrament of light. This baptismal candle in the early Church was always kept by the person baptized, and was lighted on the anniversary of one's baptism and on feast days, and brought to the church for the Easter vigil and the renewal of baptismal vows. Then later, if the person was married, the candle was lighted at his wedding. If he was ordained, it was lighted at his ordination, and when he died, it was lighted again as he went to his Judge.

The White Robe of Baptism

That the body is now the temple of God is further indicated by putting on a white robe after the Baptism itself. Today this is often only a small white cloth, but its symbolism still remains: "The body is for the Lord."

In the Transfiguration, Our Blessed Lord's garment was white (MATT. 17:2) as a symbol of holiness and purity. White was the color of the vestments in the Old Testament. It was the color of the veil which divided the sanctuary. It was the attire of the high priest. It was the color of festivity (ECCLES. 9:8), and of triumph (APOC. 6:2), and a symbol of glory and majesty (MATT. 28:3). The prayer that is said at Baptism is a petition that this garment be kept without stain: "Receive this white garment. Never let it become stained, so that when you stand before the judgment seat of Our Lord you may have life everlasting." Dante, in his practical knowledge of human nature, knowing that many do not keep it sinless, described purgatory as a "place where we go to wash our baptismal robes."

The white robe further symbolizes the recovery of the vestment of light which was man's before the Fall. As Gregory of Nyssa said: "Thou hast driven us out of paradise and called us back; Thou hast taken away the fig leaves, that garment of our misery, and clothed us once more with the robe of glory."

Because Baptism in the early Church was by immersion, there was an additional symbolism attached to the new garment that was put on, namely, to signify the entirely new life that came to one after one was "buried with Christ in His Death" (ROM. 6:4). The neophyte did not resume the clothing he had taken off. He put on a new white garment, which he wore at all services during the entire Easter octave. A week later, in the early Church, there was "the sabbath of the removal of white robes." These were solemnly taken off and deposited in the treasury of the baptismal Church.

Effects of Baptism

The first effect of Baptism is the restoration to friendship with God which was lost by original sin. The baptized person is made a partaker of the divine nature and, therefore, a sharer in divine life. There is more difference between a soul in the state of grace which begins in Baptism and a soul not in the state of grace than there is between a baptized person in the state of grace on this earth and a soul in glory in heaven. The relation of the first two is the relationship between a crystal and an elephant: one cannot beget the other. The second relationship is that of an acorn and an oak. The acorn has the potential of becoming an oak; the baptized person in grace has the potential to enjoy the glory of God. That is why Baptism is said to make the person a new creature: "In fact, when a man becomes a new creature in Christ, his old life has disappeared, everything has become new about him" (II CORINTH. 5:17).

This sharing of the divine nature makes us the adopted sons of the eternal Father. Just as Christ is the Divine Son Incarnate; so we become adopted children, as distinct from the natural Son:

> But all those who did welcome him, He empowered to become the children of God. (JOHN 1:12)

> Those who follow the leading of God's Spirit are all God's sons. (ROM. 8:14)

The Dauphin, the father of Louis XVI, gave a lesson on the effect of Baptism to his two sons. They had been baptized as infants but in emergency. It was only years later, when they had reached the age of reason, that the ceremonies were performed. Immediately after Baptism, it was noted that the names of the two children were registered after a common laborer about the palace. The royal father said:

> "See, my children, in the eyes of God, men of all conditions are equal. In His sight, faith and virtue are all that matters. One day you will be greater than this child in the eyes of the world; but if he is more virtuous than you, then he will be greater than you in the sight of God."

This likeness to God or the unlikeness will be the determinant of our future state. A mother knows her daughter is her own because that child shares her nature; a mother also knows the child next door is not her own because of the diversity of nature and parentage. So it will be with Christ on the last day. He will look into a soul and see His divine resemblance and say: "Come, ye blessed of My Father. I am the Natural Son and you are the adopted children"; but to those who have not that likeness, Christ will say: "I know you not"—and it is a terrible thing not to be known by God.

Another effect is incorporation in the Mystical Body of Christ. Baptism is not just a bond existing between the person and Christ: to be united to Christ is to be united with the Church, for the Church is His body. The Church is not an organization, but an organism. As circumcision was an incorporation into the spiritual body of Israel, so Baptism is incorporation

31

into the spiritual body of the Church. A physical body is made up of millions of cells, and all of these coordinate and cooperate into a unity, thanks to the soul which organizes them, the invisible mind which guides them, and the visible head which directs them. So too, all the baptized are incorporated into the Mystical Body, thanks to the Holy Spirit which vivifies it; thanks to the invisible head, Christ, Who rules the organism of the Church; and thanks to the visible head, its Vicar of Christ, who directs it on earth.

The two most common errors concerning the Church are these: (1) the belief that Christians came first and then the Church; and (2) that to justify the Church one must go to the New Testament—which antedated the Church.

In regard to the first error, the Christians did not come before the Church. The physical body of Christ was the beginning of the Church, and the Apostles constituted its first prolongation. The Church, or the body of Christ, was not composed of the will of individual Christians; the latter were not first brought to Our Lord and then inducted in some way into the Church. The Church has its origin not in the will of man, nor in the flesh of man, but in the will of Christ, Our Lord. The Apostles were the ministers of the Lord Himself. The world is called into the Church, but the world does not make the Church by sending men into it.

Regarding the second error, the Church was in existence throughout the entire Roman Empire, before a single book of the New Testament was written. Long before St. Paul wrote any of his epistles, he said that he had "persecuted the Church." The Church was in existence before he wrote about it so beautifully. The Gospel came out of the Church; the Church did not come out of the Gospel.

Because Baptism makes us a cell in the body of Christ, it is called the door of the Church. Each new generation of baptized Christians is taken up into that already existing unity. St. Peter, changing the analogy, describes those who are inducted into the Church as living stones:

> Draw near to Him; He is the living antitype of that stone which men rejected, which God has chosen and prized; you too must be built up on Him, stones that live and breathe, into a spiritual fabric.
>
> (I PETER 2:4, 5)

The very fact that the ceremony of Baptism begins outside of the Church, or at the door of the Church, and that the adult to be baptized is led in by a stole, confirms the fact that the unbaptized is not yet a member of the Church.

The Infusion of Virtues

Another effect is the infusion of virtues. A virtue is something like a habit. There are two kinds of habits: infused habits, such as the infused habit of swimming which a duck has when it is born; and acquired habits, such as playing the violin or speaking a foreign language.

Baptism *infuses* seven virtues into the soul, the first three of which relate to God Himself, namely, faith, hope, and charity. We are thus enabled to believe in Him, hope in Him, and love Him. But four other virtues, called moral virtues, are related to the means of attaining God; these are prudence, justice, fortitude, and temperance. By the right use of things for God's sake, by paying our debts to God, by being brave about witnessing our faith and temperate about even the legitimate pleasures of life, we reach God more quickly.

One of the reasons there is little difficulty in convincing children of the existence of God and the divinity of the Church is that they already have the gift of faith infused in their souls at the moment of Baptism. This faith, however, requires practice and intellectual fortification. If one woke up suddenly and became endowed with the gift of playing the organ, he would still have to practice to retain the gift. So, even though the gift of faith is infused, it nevertheless requires practice. In the adult, Baptism demands faith, but faith supposes that one has already received the word of God:

> "Only, how are they to call upon him until they have learned to believe in him? And how are they to believe in him, until they listen to him?"
>
> (Rom. 10:14)

It may be asked why adults who already have the faith are said to need Baptism. If the adult is already justified by faith, Baptism is necessary in order that he may be incorporated visibly and sacramentally to Christ in His Church. Furthermore, they receive, in virtue of Baptism, a *fuller grace*. In the case of children, the habit of virtue becomes a conscious act later on. The faith is not just a profession of doctrine, but is the commitment to Our Lord and Savior.

Another effect, which is closely bound up with grace, is the indwelling of the Trinity in our souls, from which arises a triple relationship with the Godhead. First is the relationship with *God the Father*. The baptized may now say "Our Father." By nature, we are only creatures of God; by Baptism, we are sons:

> The spirit you have now received is not, as of old, a spirit of
> slavery, to govern you by fear; it is the spirit of adoption, which
> makes us cry out, Abba, Father.
>
> (ROM. 8:15)

We also have relationship with the Son of God, Who is "the firstborn
of many brethren" (ROM. 8:29). The baptized person will, therefore, try
to reproduce in his soul the image of Christ. As it is put in *Imitation of
Christ:*

> Who will give me, Lord, to find You and You alone, and to offer
> You my whole heart . . . You in me, and I in You, and therefore
> together, evermore to dwell.

Finally, there is union with the Holy Spirit. At the moment of Baptism
the priest says, "Depart, unclean spirit, and give place to the Holy Spirit."
St. John writes: "This is our proof that we are dwelling in Him and He
in us; He has given us a share of His own Spirit" (I JOHN 4:13). The Spirit
within us is a moving Spirit, illumining the mind and strengthening the
will to sanctify ourselves and others:

> Nor does this hope delude us; the love of God has been poured
> out in our hearts by the Holy Spirit, whom we have received.
>
> (ROM. 5:4)

The world, therefore, is divided into the "once born" and the "twice
born": between the sons of the old Adam, and the sons of the new Adam,
Christ; between the unregenerate and the regenerate. There is a real in-
equality in the world. There are "superior" and "inferior" peoples, but the
basis of distinction is not color, race, nationality, or wealth. The superior
people of the earth are the supermen, the Godmen; the inferior people are
those who have been called to that superior state but, as yet, have not
embraced it. But the reborn must follow the laws of divine life, for which
the Lord has prepared other sacraments.

II

THE SACRAMENT
OF CONFIRMATION

In the biological order, a creature must first be born, then it must grow. In the supernatural order of grace, divine life is born in the soul by Baptism; then it must grow "in age and grace and wisdom before God and men." The soul who receives the sacraments of Baptism and Confirmation is born spiritually and matures spiritually. It receives citizenship in the Kingdom of God and is inducted into God's spiritual army and the lay priesthood of believers. This soul is "born of the Virgin Mary"—the Church—and begins its apostolate as Our Lord began his preaching after the descent of the Holy Spirit at His baptism in the Jordan.

Confirmation, like every other sacrament, is modeled upon Christ, and reaffirms some aid or gesture in His life. It is bound up with Our Lord's Baptism in the Jordan when the Holy Spirit descended upon Him in the form of a dove.

Our Lord had a double priestly anointing corresponding to two aspects of His life: the first, the Incarnation, made Him capable of becoming a victim for our sins, because He then had a body with which He could suffer. As God He could not suffer; as Man He could. This first aspect culminated in the Passion and Resurrection, which one participates in by Baptism.

But the sacrament of Confirmation is particularly a participation in the second anointing of Our Lord, that of the coming of the Spirit in the Jordan, which ordained Him to the mission of preaching the apostolate. This reached its culmination on Pentecost, when He filled His Church—His Mystical Body—with His Spirit. Pentecost is to the New Testament what the gift of the law is to the Old Testament, only it is more perfect.

The descent of the Holy Spirit on Christ in the Jordan had a double effect on Our Lord. It prepared Him for combat:

> Jesus returned from the Jordan full of the Holy Spirit, and by the Spirit He was led on into the wilderness, where He remained forty days, tempted by the devil.
>
> (LUKE 4:1)

It prepared Him for preaching the Kingdom of God:

> The Spirit of the Lord is upon me; He has anointed me, and sent me out to preach the gospel to the poor, to restore the broken-hearted; to bid the prisoners go free, and the blind to have sight; to set the oppressed at liberty, to proclaim a year when men may find acceptance with the Lord.
>
> (LUKE 4:18, 19)

About three years later, at the Last Supper, Our Blessed Lord promised to send the Spirit to His Apostles, disciples, and followers, which He did fifty days after the Resurrection on Pentecost. It would seem better if Our Lord had remained on earth, so that all ages might have heard His voice and thrilled to the majesty of His person; but He said it was better that He leave, otherwise the Spirit would not come. If He remained on earth, He would have been only an example to be copied, but if He sent the Holy Spirit, He would be a life to be lived.

Though Our Lord knew on Holy Thursday that His Apostles were distressed because He spoke of His approaching death, He consoled them with the advantages of His leaving this earth and yet remaining in it, in another way:

> So full are your hearts with sorrow at My telling you this. And yet I can say truly that it is better for you I should go away; he who is to befriend you will not come to you unless I do go, but if only I make my way there, I will send him to you.
>
> (JOHN 16:6, 7)

36

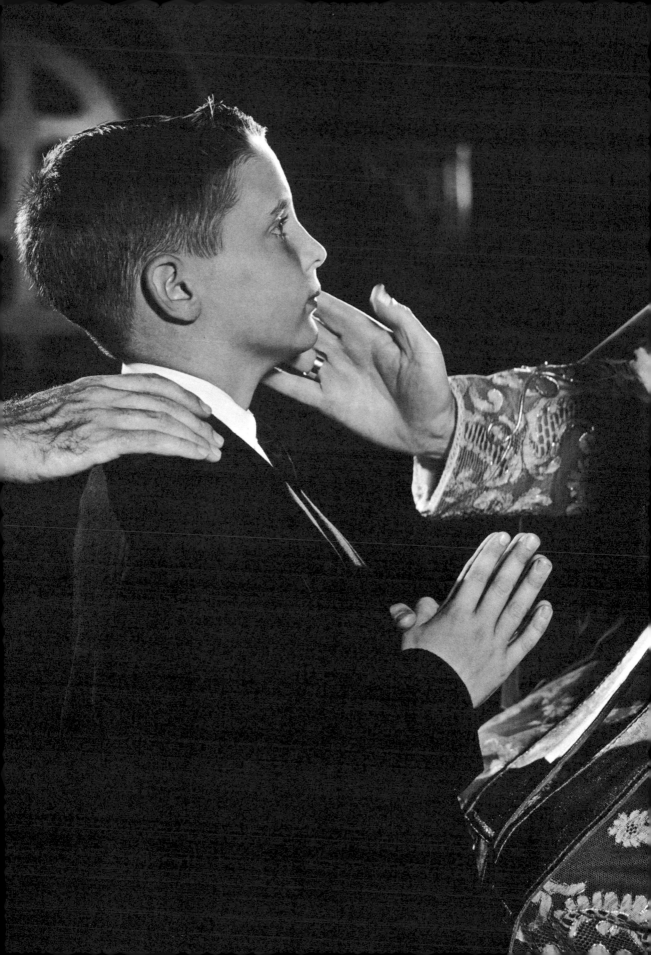

His perpetual presence, even in His glorified state, would have limited His moral and spiritual influence. He might have become to man the type of Christ that Hollywood presents—a celebrity. Instead of being in our hearts, He would only have been in our senses.

Would men ever have thought of spiritual fellowship with Christ, when physical fellowship might be had; when good and bad would have had equal perception of Him; when He would be external to the soul of man, not internal? Where would faith be, if we saw? And would not the world have tried to recrucify Him, though that would have been impossible after His Resurrection?

These questions are in vain; Divine Wisdom said it was better that He depart from the globe for, once in glory, He would send His Spirit, "the Truth-giving Spirit to guide you in all Truth." Great men influence the earth only from their funeral urns; but He, Who gave the earth the only serious wound it ever received—the empty tomb—would rule it at the right hand of the Father through His Spirit.

This Spirit He sent upon the Church on Pentecost, like a soul entering a fetus; chemicals which are disparate and disconnected became a living thing. So the Apostles, with their individual whims and ignorances, were, under the pentecostal fires, fused into the visible, living, Mystical Body of Christ. It is not to the point in a book on the sacraments to describe this; but it is to the point to say that Confirmation is a kind of Pentecost to a baptized soul. Christ dwelling in the flesh would normally be in one place only at one time, but His Spirit, unbound by fleshy bonds, could cover the earth, working on a million hearts at once. Nor would such hearts be without comfort at His physical absence, for the Spirit He called "another Comforter."

It is the Son, Christ Our Lord, Who reveals the Heavenly Father. We would never know the mercy and love of the Father, if He had not sent His Son to walk this earth and pay our debt for sin. But who reveals the Son? It is the Holy Spirit.

We know what goes on in other minds because we, too, have minds or souls; we know what goes on in the mind of Christ because we are given His Spirit. The natural or unbaptized man cannot perceive the things of God, for they are spiritually discerned. As the scientist knows nature, so the Christian, thanks to the Spirit, knows Christ:

> He will not utter a message of His own; he will utter the message that has been given to Him; and He will make plain to you what is still to come. And He will bring honor to me, because it is from me that He will derive what He makes plain to you. I

say that He will derive from me what He makes plain to you, because all that belongs to the Father belongs to me.

(JOHN 16:13–15)

It is through the Spirit received in Confirmation that Christ walks the earth again in each obedient Christian; it is through the Spirit that we are sanctified, comforted, and taught to pray.

These and other words of Our Lord about sending the Spirit of Truth who will enlarge our knowledge of Him, prove that the whole truth is not available to us in written records. Pentecost was not the descent of a book, but of living tongues of fire. Confirmation gives the lie to those who say that "the sermon on the mount is enough for them." Our Lord's teaching, as recorded in the Gospels, was implemented, complemented, and revealed in its deeper meaning through the spirit of truth He gave to His Church. We indeed know Christ by reading the Gospels, but we see the deeper meaning of the words, and we know Christ more completely when we have His Spirit. It is only through the Spirit that we know He is the divine Son of God and Redeemer of humanity:

> Those who live the life of nature cannot be acceptable to God;
> but you live the life of the spirit, not the life of nature; that is, if
> the Spirit of God dwells in you. A man cannot belong to Christ
> unless he has the Spirit of Christ.
>
> (ROM. 8:8, 9)

Because an added measure of the Spirit is given in Confirmation, it was administered, even in the early Church, not by disciples but by Apostles or by the bishops who had the fullness of the priesthood.

The deacon Philip went to a city of Samaria and preached Christ to them. He converted and baptized many. But, in order to "lay hands on them" or confirm them, it was necessary for the Church in Jerusalem to send Peter and John (ACTS 8:5–17). Later on we read about Confirmation at Ephesus by the Apostle Paul: "When Paul laid his hands on them, the Holy Spirit came upon them" (ACTS 19:6).

Administration of the Sacrament

The candidates kneel with hands joined before the bishop, who, extending his hands over the ones to be confirmed, says:

> Almighty, everlasting God, Who has deigned to beget new life
> in these thy servants by water and the Holy Spirit, and has
> granted them remission of all their sins, send forth from heaven
> upon them Thy Holy Spirit, with His sevenfold gifts: The spirit

of wisdom and understanding. Amen. The spirit of counsel and fortitude. Amen. The spirit of knowledge and piety. Amen. Fill them with the spirit of fear of the Lord, and seal them with the sign of Christ's cross, plenteous in mercy unto life everlasting. Through the selfsame Jesus Christ, Thy Son, Our Lord, Who liveth and reigneth with Thee in the unity of the Holy Spirit, God eternally. Amen.

Dipping his thumb in holy chrism, he confirms the person saying:

> [Name] I confirm thee with the chrism of salvation. In the name of the Father [making the sign of the cross] and of the Son [making the sign of the cross] and of the Holy Spirit [making the sign of the cross].

Then he gives the one confirmed a slight blow on the cheek, saying, "Peace be to you."

Other prayers and a penance follow, all of which are destined to make the Christian a witness, a teacher to an unbelieving world, and even a martyr, if need be, for the Church. Two of the effects and obligations of the Church deserve special consideration, and this follows.

The Sacrament of Combat

Every sacrament is related to the death of Christ, but Confirmation intensifies that resemblance. Baptism gives the Christian a treasure; Confirmation urges him to fight to preserve it against the three great enemies: the world, the flesh, and the devil.

The military character of the sacrament is evidenced in the following four symbols or acts:

(1) *The forehead is anointed with chrism in the sign of the cross.* The cross, by its nature, evokes opposition. The more one crucifies his passions and rejects the false teachings of the world, the more he is slandered and attacked. Calvary united not only the friends of Our Lord; it also united His enemies. Those who were opposed to one another merged their lesser conflicts for the sake of the greater hate. Judas and the Sanhedrin, Pharisees and Publicans, religious courts and Roman overlords—though they despised one another, nevertheless they rained common blows of hammer and nails on the hands and feet of Christ:

> It is because you do not belong to the world, because I have singled you out from the midst of the world, that the world hates you. (JOHN 15:18, 19)

41

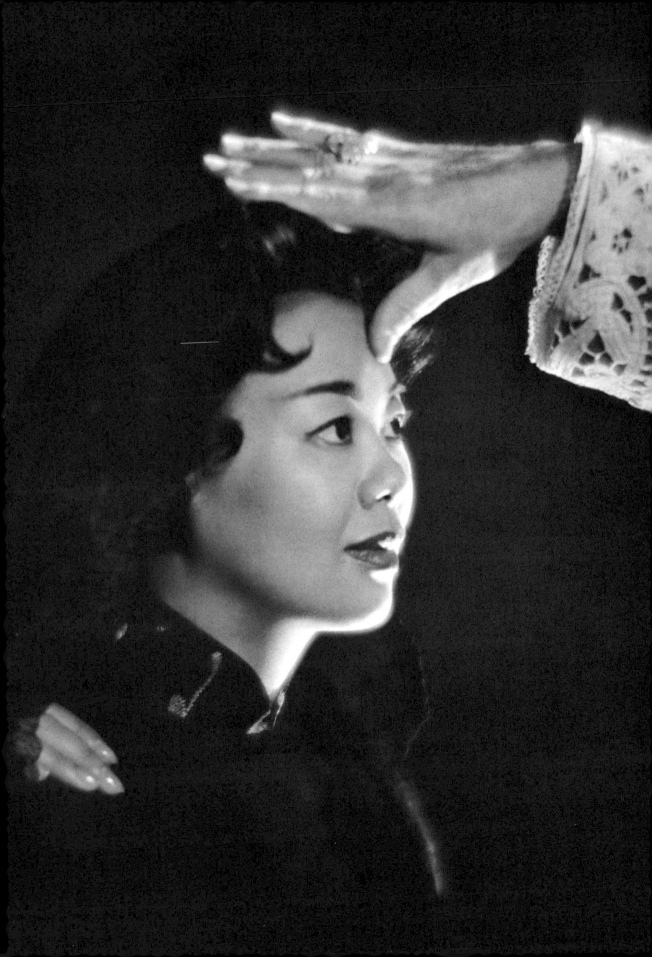

When the Little Flower, St. Thérése, prepared herself for Confirmation, she saw that it implied crucifixion:

> I went into retreat for Confirmation. I carefully prepared myself for the coming of the Holy Spirit. I cannot understand why so little attention is paid to the sacrament of love. Like the Apostles, I happily awaited the promised Comforter. I rejoiced that soon I should be a perfect Christian, and have eternally marked upon my forehead the mysterious Cross of this ineffable sacrament. On that day I received the strength to suffer, a strength which I much needed, for the martyrdom of my soul was about to begin.

(2) *The interior grace of the sacrament gives fortitude and other gifts destined for the battle of the Spirit.* The Apostles on Pentecost were made *witnesses* to the Resurrection of Christ, and the word *witness* in Greek means *martyr*. So, in Confirmation, the Christian is marked with power and boldness on the forehead, so that neither fear nor false modesty will deter him from the public confession of Christ. Cattle are often branded with the owner's name; and slaves or soldiers in the emperor's service were tattooed so that they could be easily recognized if they ever deserted the service. Plutarch states it was a custom to brand cattle that were destined for sacrifice, as a sign that they were set apart for something sacred. Herodotus tells of a temple in Egypt in which a fugitive might take the right of sanctuary: once he did so, he was stamped, marked, or tattooed as an indication that he was the property of God and, therefore, was inviolable and sacrosanct.

The spiritual significance of marking is anticipated: ". . . all alike destroy till none is left, save only where you see the cross marked upon them" (EZECHIAL 9:6). On the last day, the elect will be sealed on their foreheads in the name of the Lamb and of His Father, to protect them from destruction (APOC. 7:3). Confirmation, then, is the sealing of a person in the army of the Lord. St. Paul says: "Do not distress God's Holy Spirit, whose seal you bear until the day of your redemption comes" (EPH. 4:30).

(3) *A slight blow on the cheek is given the person confirmed to remind him that, as a soldier of Christ, he must be prepared to suffer all things for His sake.* To deny one's faith for a passing carnal pleasure, or to surrender it under ridicule, is far more serious in the eyes of God than a soldier deserting his duty. Péguy, bemoaning a want of spiritual bravery, writes:

> Shame upon those who are ashamed. It is not a question of believing or not believing; it is a question of knowing what is the

43

most frequent cause of loss of faith. No cause can be more shameful than shame—and fear. And of all the fears the most shameful is certainly the fear of ridicule; the fear of being taken for a fool. One may believe, or one may not believe. But shame upon him who would deny his God to avoid being made a mark for witticisms. I have in mind the poor, timorous wretch who looks fearfully on every side to be sure that there is not some high personage who has laughed at him, at his faith, at his God. Shame upon the ashamed. Shame implies a cowardice that has nothing to fall back upon. Shame upon those who are ashamed.

(4) *The combative character of Confirmation is further shown by the fact that its ordinary minister is the bishop, who is, as it were, a general in the military of the Church.* Because Confirmation gives an increase of the Holy Spirit over Baptism, it is fittingly administered by the one who has the fullness of the priesthood. When the bishop extends his arms over those confirmed, as a successor of the Apostles, he imitates Peter and John who laid hands on new converts of Samaria, so that "they received the Holy Spirit" (ACTS 8:1). He also imitates Paul at Ephesus: "When Paul laid his hands on them, the Holy Spirit came upon them" (ACTS 19:6). The bishop is not a hoarder of his authority; he is a dispenser of it, as was Our Blessed Lord Who told His Apostles that they were to make disciples of all nations (MATT. 18:19–20).

The bishop, as the authority in the Church, incorporates the one confirmed into *adult* responsibilities. From now on, the one confirmed does not lead an individual Christian life: he becomes commissioned in the army. Confirmation is, therefore, the first great manifestation of the relation established between the authority of the Church and Christian personality.

Confirmation Both Personal and Social

Every sacrament has been set as a kind of balance between the individual and the community. The individual is baptized, but his Baptism incorporates him into the community of believers—the Church. The grace descends into the soul of the individual, but the grace is for the perfection of the Mystical Body. This is true also of the sacrament of Confirmation for, even more than Baptism, it orients us toward the community or fellowship of believers. Love is a union by which one escapes from egotism. When one reaches spiritual adulthood, one is open for a wider love. Children live for themselves; adults cease to live exclusively for themselves, particularly those who reach the "perfect age" in the spirit. The combat of

44

Baptism was, we said, a *personal* combat: in Confirmation, the combat is *ex officio* military, and under the orders of the chief. Baptism is principally the battle against invisible enemies: in Confirmation, it is the battle against social enemies, such as the persecutors of the Church.

The mystical death one undergoes in Baptism is individual: in Confirmation, the mystical death is communal. We are prepared to die, to be a martyr, or a witness to Christ for the sake of the "body which is the Church." Confirmation then relates us to the community; that is why the Spirit was given on Pentecost when all the Apostles were assembled together with Mary in their midst.

Confirmation makes us soldiers of Christ. Soldiers do not come together of and by themselves to constitute an army. Rather, it is the political authority of government which summons the soldiers and constitutes them as an army. So it is in Confirmation. The Church does not have a spiritual military because her members volunteer for service. It is rather that the Church makes them grow spiritually to a point where they can carry spiritual arms and be authorized as her combatants bearing the "breastplate of justice fitted on . . . the shield of faith . . . the helmet of salvation . . . and the sword of the spirit" (EPH. 6:14, 16, 17).

The Sacrament of the Lay Apostolate

The laity are summoned by Confirmation to share in the apostolate of the Church, to be witnesses to Christ before those who know Him not, to be prophets or teachers in an unbelieving world and, together with the priesthood, to offer their bodies as a reasonable sacrifice to the Heavenly Father:

> You are a chosen race, a royal priesthood, a consecrated nation,
> a people God means to have for Himself; it is yours to proclaim
> the exploits of the God Who has called you out of darkness into
> His marvelous light.
>
> (I PETER 2:9)

The laity share in the general priesthood of the Church because all are members of Jesus the priest; but they do not share in the ministerial or hierarchical priesthood which comes with Holy Orders, in which there is a *personal* representation of Christ, such as offering the eucharistic sacrifice and absolving sins.

The laity have a double consecration through Baptism and Confirmation, which gives them a certain participation in the priesthood of Christ.

45

The ministerial or hierarchical priesthood, however, has the third and specific consecration from Holy Orders. There are thus two sorts of priesthood: the first is *external* and reserved for the hierarchical priesthood; the second is *internal* and common to all the faithful.

The person who is confirmed always has a personal and, in some instances, a canonical mission. He has a personal mission inasmuch as, through his own personal contact, he must help bring other souls to Christ—just as Andrew brought Peter, Philip brought Nathaniel, the Samaritan woman brought her townspeople, and Philip converted the eunuch of the Ethiopian court.

But the mission given by Confirmation requires a wider outlook than the personal work of witnessing and converting. It is not only individual souls, but also the milieu, the environment—the whole social order in all its political, scientific, journalistic, medical, legal, recreational, and economic structures which also has to be Christianized.

This canonical mission of spiritualizing the world in an organized way is dependent on the hierarchy and the teaching authority of the Church. There is some communication of this teaching office in the ceremony of the imposition of hands. The laity do not participate in the hierarchy, but they participate in the apostolate of the hierarchy. The Apostles and their successors have a divine mission to teach; the laity receive from the hierarchy a canonical mission to teach.

What makes Catholic Action is not the fact that Catholics are organized, but that they have received a mission to bear witness to Christ over and above their own personal witnessing to Christ in the holiness of their lives. The laity are not just the Church taught; they participate in the Church teaching. As Leo XIII said, the laity cannot arrogate to themselves this authority, but when circumstances demand it, they have the right to communicate to others, as echoes of the magisterium of the Church, that which they themselves have learned. And Pope Pius XII addressed a new group of cardinals as follows:

> The laity must have an ever clearer consciousness, not only of belonging to the Church, but of being the Church; that is, of being the community of the faithful on earth under the guidance of their common leader, the Pope, and the bishops in communion with him. *They are the Church.*

The Acts of Apostles twice shows that when the disciples were scattered by persecution, the laity immediately began to preach God's word and increase the Church (ACTS 8:4, ACTS 9:19), something that is happening

46

today in persecuted lands. Aquilla and his wife, Priscilla, completed the instructions of Apollos (ACTS 18:26), and later on became the trusted helpers of St. Paul (ROM. 16:3). Apollos, who never seems to have received any ministerial consecration, was a vigorous preacher of Christ (ACTS 18:27, 28).

There have even been laymen who taught theology. For example, John d'Andrea was professor of canon law at Bologna from 1302 to 1348. Wilfred G. Ward was professor of dogmatic theology at St. Edmund's Seminary of London, England, from 1851 to 1858.

More and more, the Church is emphasizing the teaching mission conferred by Confirmation. In mission lands, catechists number tens of thousands. Abroad and at home, the canonical mission of teaching is conferred implicitly on teachers when the bishops appoint them to parochial schools.

III

THE SACRAMENT OF THE EUCHARIST

A young wife, who had been taking instructions for a year, told the writer she could believe everything in the faith except the Eucharist. Upon inquiring about her husband, it was learned that he was in the Pacific on military duty. In answer to further questions, she admitted that she corresponded with him every two days and that she had his photograph before her in the house.

We argued there was nothing wanting for perfect happiness. What more could she want than the constant memory of him through the photograph and a written communication in which heart poured out to heart. But she protested that she could never be truly happy except through union with her husband.

But, it was retorted, if human love craves oneness, shall not divine love? If husband and wife seek to be one in the flesh, shall not the Christian and Christ crave for that oneness with one another? The memory of the Christ who lived twenty centuries ago, the recalling of His mercy and miracles through memory, the correspondence with Him by reading the Scriptures—all these are satisfying, but they do not satisfy love. There must be, on the level of grace, something unitive with divine love. Every

49

heart seeks a happiness outside it, and since perfect love is God, then the heart of man and the heart of Christ must, in some way, fuse. In human friendship the other person is loved as another self, or the other half of one's soul. Divine friendship must have its mutual "indwelling": "He who dwells in love dwells in God and God in him" (I JOHN 4:17). This aspiration of the soul for its ecstasy is fulfilled in the Sacrament of the Eucharist.

The Eucharist: Sacrifice and Sacrament

The Sacrament of the Eucharist has two sides: it is both a *sacrifice* and a *sacrament*. Inasmuch as biological life is nothing but a reflection, a dim echo, and a shadow of the divine life, one can find analogies in the natural order for the beauties of the divine. Does not nature itself have a double aspect: a sacrifice and a sacrament? The vegetables which are served at table, the meat which is presented on the platter, are the natural sacraments of the body of man. By them he lives. If they were endowed with speech, they would say: "Unless you have communion with me, you will not live."

But if one inquires as to how the lower creation of chemicals, vegetables or meats came to be the sacrament or the communion of man, one is immediately introduced to the idea of sacrifice. Did not the vegetables have to be pulled up by their roots from the earth, submitted to the law of death, and then pass through the ordeal of fire before they could become the sacrament of physical life, or have communion with the body? Was not the meat on the platter once a living thing, and was it not submitted to the knife, its blood shed on the soil of a natural Gethsemane and Calvary before it was fit to be presented to man?

Nature, therefore, suggests that a *sacrifice must precede a sacrament;* death is the prelude to a communion. In some way, unless the thing dies, it does not begin to live in a higher kingdom. To have, for example, a communion service without a sacrifice would be, in the natural order, like eating our vegetables uncooked, and our meat in the raw. When we come face to face with the realities of life, we see that *we live by what we slay.* Elevating this to the supernatural order, we still live by what we slay. It was our sins that slew Christ on Calvary, and yet by the power of God risen from the dead and reigning gloriously in Heaven, He now becomes our life and has communion with us and we with Him. In the divine order, there must be the Sacrifice or the Consecration of the Mass before there can be the sacrament or the Communion of the soul and God.

50

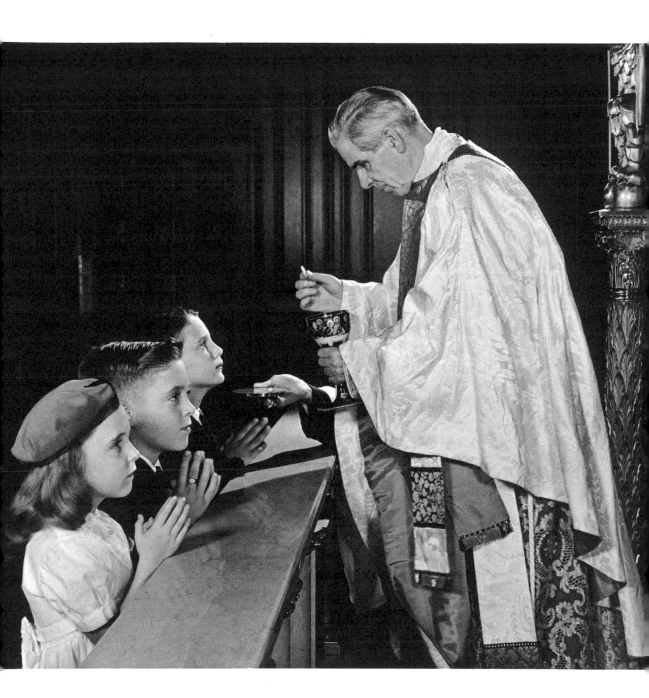

Relation of Baptism and the Eucharist

Baptism is the initiation to the Christian life, and corresponds in the biological order to the beginning of life. But the birth to Divine Life comes only through a death; that is to say, an immersion under water which mystically symbolizes dying and being buried with Christ. The Eucharist is a sacrifice; it also incorporates us to the Death of Christ. Baptism, however, is a more *passive* representation of that death, particularly in an infant, where the will of the infant does not submit to it, except through the sponsors. The Eucharist is a much more *active* representation of the death of Christ because the Mass is an unbloody presentation of the sacrificial death of Christ outside the walls of Jerusalem.

The Fathers of the Church were constantly struck by the relationship between Baptism and the Eucharist; the blood and the water which flowed from the side of Christ on the Cross had deep significance. Water was the symbol of our regeneration and, therefore, betokened Baptism; blood, the price of our Redemption, was the sign of the Eucharist.

This brings up the question, if there is a relationship to the death of Christ in both sacraments, what is the difference between them? One of the differences is that in Baptism and the other sacraments, except the Eucharist, we are united to Christ simply by a participation of His grace, but in the Eucharist, Christ exists substantially, and is really and truly present—Body, Blood, Soul and Divinity. In the Eucharist, man realizes more fully his incorporation to the Death and Resurrection of Christ than in Baptism. In the physical order, birth always gives resemblance to parents; but when a mother nourishes her child, there is a new bond established between the child and the mother. So in Baptism, there is a resemblance to the Divine nature created, inasmuch as we are made "other Christs"; but in the Eucharist, we receive the very substance of Christ Himself. Because of the close relationship between the two sacraments, the Council of Mayence in 1549 directed pastors to administer Baptism in the morning during the course of the Mass, or at least as soon after Mass as possible.

There is somewhat the same relationship existing between Baptism and the Eucharist, as there is between faith and charity or perfect love. Baptism is the sacrament of faith, because it is the foundation of the spiritual life. The Eucharist is the sacrament of charity or love because it is the re-enactment of the perfect act of love of Christ; namely, His death on the Cross and the giving of Himself to us in Holy Communion.

52

The Old Testament and the Eucharist

It would take pages to reveal the prefigurement of the Sacrament of the Eucharist in the Old Testament. Melchisedech offering bread and wine was a figure of Christ Himself, Who chose bread and wine the night of the Last Supper as the elements for both the sacrifice and the sacrament. The manna that fell in the desert was also a symbol of the Eucharist, which Our Blessed Lord said was Himself: "I myself am the living bread that has come down from heaven" (JOHN 5:51). St. Paul, picking up the analogy, said that what the Jews ate in the desert was a figure of our spiritual food: "They all ate the same prophetic food. . . . It is we that were foreshadowed in these events" (I CORINTH. 10:3, 6).

The blood of the paschal lamb, sprinkled on doorposts to preserve the Jews from destruction, was a sign not yet of a reality, but a figure of the blood of Christ sprinkled on our souls, which would save us from evil. Because the paschal lamb was a figure of Christ, it was on the feast of the Passover that Our Blessed Lord gave to His Church the Eucharist which He had promised over a year before at Capharnaum.

The Eucharist as a Sacrifice, or the Mass

The Mass has three important parts: the Offertory, the Consecration, and the Communion. In the order of human love, these correspond to engagement, the marriage ceremony, and the consummation of the marriage. When a man becomes engaged to a woman, he generally brings her the gift of a precious ring; it is not of tin or straw, because these represent no sacrifice. Regardless of how much he might pay for the ring, he would still tear off the price tag, in order that his beloved might never establish any correspondence between the price of the gift and his love. No matter how much he gave her, the gift to him would seem inadequate. The ring is round in order to express the eternity of his love which has neither beginning nor end; it is precious, because it is a symbol of the total readiness to give his whole personality to the beloved.

The Mass, too, has an engagement which corresponds to the Offertory of the Mass, in which the faithful bring gifts of bread and wine, or its equivalent, that which buys bread and wine. As the ring is a symbol of the lover offering himself to the beloved, so too, the bread and wine are the symbols of a person offering himself to Christ. This is apparent in several ways: first, since bread and wine have traditionally nourished man

and given him life, in bringing that which was the substance of his life, he is equivalently giving himself. Second, the readiness to sacrifice himself for the beloved is revealed in the bread and wine; no two substances have to undergo more to become what they are than do wheat and grapes. One passes through the Gethsemane of a mill, the other through the Calvary of the winepress before they can be presented to the Beloved on the altar. In the Offertory, therefore, under the appearance of bread and wine, the faithful are offering themselves to Christ.

After the engagement comes the marriage ceremony in which the lover sacrifices himself for the beloved, and the beloved surrenders devotedly to the lover. The groom practically says, "My greatest freedom is to be your slave. I give up my individuality in order to serve you." The joining of hands in the marriage ceremony is a symbol of the transfer of self to another self: "I am yours and you are mine. I want to die to myself, in order to live in you, my beloved. I cannot live unto you, unless I give up myself. So I say to you, 'This is My Body; this is My Blood'."

In the Mass, the faithful are already present on the altar under the appearance of bread and wine. At the moment of the Consecration of the Mass, when the priest as Christ pronounces the words "This is My Body" and "This is My Blood," the substance of the bread becomes the substance of the body of Christ, and the substance of the wine becomes the substance of the blood of Christ. At that moment, the faithful are saying in a secondary sense with the priest: "This is *my* body; this is *my* blood. Take it! I no longer want it for myself. The very substance of my being, my intellect, and my will—change! Transubstantiate!—so that my ego is lost in Thee, so that my intellect is one with Thy Truth, and my will is one with Thy desires! I care not if the species or appearances of my life remain; that is to say, my duties, my avocation, my appointments in time and space. But what I am substantially, I give to Thee."

In the human order, after the engagement and the marriage is the consummation of the marriage. All love craves unity. Correspondence by letter, or by speech, cannot satisfy that instinctive yearning of two hearts to be lost in one another. There must, therefore, come some great ecstatic moment in which love becomes too deep for words; this is the communion of body and blood with body and blood in the oneness which lasts not long, but is a foretaste of Heaven.

The marital act is nothing but a fragile and shadowy image of Communion in which, after having offered ourselves under the appearance of bread and wine and having died to our lower self, we now begin to enjoy that ecstatic union with Christ in Holy Communion—a oneness which is, in the language of Thompson, "a passionless passion, a wild tranquility." This is the moment when the hungry heart communes with the Bread of Life; this is the rapture in which is fulfilled that "love we fall just short of in all love," and that rapture that leaves all other raptures pain.

The Sacrifice of the Mass may be presented under another analogy. Picture a house which had two large windows on opposite sides. One window looks down into a valley, the other to a towering mountain. The owner could gaze on both and somehow see that they were related: the valley is the mountain humbled; the mountain is the valley exalted.

The Sacrifice of the Mass is something like that. Every church, in a way, looks down on a valley, but the valley of death and humiliation in which we see a cross. But it also looks up to a mountain, an eternal mountain, the mountain of heaven where Christ reigns gloriously. As the valley and the mountain are related as humiliation and exaltation, so the Sacrifice of the Mass is related to Calvary in the valley, and to Christ in heaven and the eternal hills.

All three, Calvary, the Mass, and the glorified Christ in heaven are different levels of the great eternal act of love. The Christ Who appeared in heaven as the lamb slain from the beginning of the world, at a certain moment in time, came to this earth and offered His Life in Redemption for the sins of men. Then He ascended into heaven where that same eternal act of love continues, as He intercedes for humanity, showing the scars of His Love to His heavenly Father. True, agony and crucifixion are passing things, but the obedience and the love which inspired them are not. In the Father's eyes, the Son-made-Man loves always unto death. The patriot who regretted that he had only one life to give to his country, would have loved to have made his sacrifice eternal. Being man, he could not do it. But Christ, being God and man, could.

The Mass, therefore, looks backward and forward. Because we live in time and can use only earthly symbols, we see successively that which is but one eternal movement of love. If a motion picture reel were endowed with consciousness, it would see and understand the story at once; but we do not grasp it until we see it unfolded upon the screen. So it is with the love by which Christ prepared for His coming in the Old Testament, offered Himself on Calvary, and now re-presents it in Sacrifice in the Mass. The Mass, therefore, is not another immolation but a new presentation of the eternal Victim and its application to us. To assist at Mass is the same as to assist at Calvary. But there are differences.

On the Cross, Our Lord offered Himself for all mankind; in the Mass we make application of that death to ourselves, and unite our sacrifice with His. The disadvantage of not having lived at the time of Christ is nullified

56

by the Mass. On the Cross, He *potentially* redeemed all humanity; in the Mass we actualize that Redemption. Calvary happened at a definite moment in time and on a particular hill in space. The Mass temporalizes and spatializes that eternal act of love.

The Sacrifice of Calvary was offered up in a bloody manner by the separation of His blood from His body. In the Mass, this death is mystically and sacramentally presented in an unbloody manner, by the separate consecration of bread and wine. The two are not consecrated together by such words as "This is My Body and My Blood"; rather, following the words of Our Lord: "This is My Body" is said over the bread; then, "This is My Blood" is said over the wine. The separate consecration is a kind of mystical sword dividing body and blood, which is the way Our Lord died on Calvary.

Suppose there was an eternal broadcasting station that sent out eternal waves of wisdom and enlightenment. People who lived in different ages would tune in to that wisdom, assimilate it, and apply it to themselves. Christ's eternal act of love is something to which we tune in, as we appear in successive ages of history through the Mass. The Mass, therefore, borrows its reality and its efficacy from Calvary and has no meaning apart from it. He who assists at Mass lifts the Cross of Christ out of the soil of Calvary and plants it in the center of his own heart.

This is the only perfect act of love, sacrifice, thanksgiving, and obedience which we can ever pay to God; namely, that which is offered by His Divine Son Incarnate. Of and by ourselves, we cannot touch the ceiling because we are not tall enough. Of and by ourselves, we cannot touch God. We need a Mediator, someone who is both God and Man, Who is Christ. No human prayer, no human act of self-denial, no human sacrifice is sufficient to pierce Heaven. It is only the Sacrifice of the Cross that can do so, and this is done in the Mass. As we offer it, we hang, as it were, onto His robes, we tug at His feet at the Ascension, we cling to His pierced hands in offering Himself to the Heavenly Father. Being hidden in Him, our prayers and sacrifices have His value. In the Mass we are once more at Calvary, rubbing shoulders with Mary Magdalen and John, while mournfully looking over our shoulders at executioners who still shake dice for the garments of the Lord.

The priest who offers the Sacrifice merely lends to Christ his voice and his fingers. It is Christ Who is the Priest; it is Christ Who is the Victim. In all pagan sacrifices and in the Jewish sacrifices, the victim was always *separate* from the priest. It might have been a goat, a lamb, or a bullock. But when Christ came, He the Priest offered Himself as the Victim. In the Mass, it is Christ Who still offers Himself and Who is the Victim to Whom we become united. The altar, therefore, is not related to the congregation as the stage to an audience in the theatre. The communion rail is not the same as footlights, which divide the drama from the onlooker. All the members of the Church have a kind of priesthood, inasmuch as they offer up with the Eternal Priest this eternal act of love. The laity participate in the life and power of Christ, for "Thou hast made us a royal race of priests to serve God" (Apoc. 5:10).

The expression, sometimes used by Catholics "to hear Mass," is an indication of how little is understood of their active participation, not only with Christ, but also with all of the saints and members of the Church until the end of time. This corporate action of the Church is indicated in certain prayers of the Mass. For example, immediately before the Consecration, God is asked to receive the offering which "we Thy servants and Thy whole household make unto Thee"; and after the Consecration the faithful again say, "We Thy servants, as also Thy holy people, do offer unto Thy most excellent majesty of Thine own gifts bestowed on us." All participate, but the closer we are to the mystery, the more we become one with Christ.

No man can ever come to the real fullness of his personality by reflection or contemplation; he has to *act it out*. That is why through all ages man laid his hand on the best of the herd and destroyed it in order to indicate the offering and surrender of himself. By laying his hands on the animal, he identified himself with it. Then he consumed it, in order to gain some identification with the one to whom it was offered. In the Mass, all the ancient dim foreshadowings of the supreme sacrifice are fulfilled. Man immolates himself with Christ, bidding Him to take his body and his blood. Through this destruction of the ego, there is a void and an emptiness created, which makes it possible for Divinity to fill up the vacuum and to make the offerer holy. Man dies to the past, in order that he may live in the future. He chooses to be united with his Divine King in some form of death, that he may share in His Resurrection and glory. Thus dying he lives; chastened he is not killed; sorrowful he always rejoices; giving up time, he finds eternity. Nothingness is exchanged for everything. Poverty turns into riches, and having nothing, he begins to possess all things.

The Eucharist as a Sacrament, or Holy Communion

Running through the universe is the law that nothing lives unless it consumes. Plant life, obedient to this law, goes down to the earth, eats and drinks from it its waters, phosphates, and carbonates, and circulates them through its organism. The animal, because endowed with a higher life than that of the plant, is in still greater need of nourishment. It needs not

only the nourishment of the mineral order, the air, the sunlight and the like, but also the nourishment of plant life. The instinct of the animal is to seek food. The animal roaming in the field, the fish swimming in the water, the eagle soaring in the air, all are in search of daily bread, for without knowing it, they acknowledge that life is impossible without nourishment, that life grows only by life, and that the joy of living comes from communion with another kind of life.

Because men, as well as animals, have bodies, they are under the necessity of feeding these bodies. The food for which they clamor is more delicate because the human body is more delicate. The body is not content, as the plant, to take its food from the ground, raw, uncooked, and unseasoned. It seeks the refinement that comes with a higher creature but in doing so, acknowledges the law that every living thing must nourish itself.

Man has a soul, as well as a body. The spiritual part of him demands a food which is above the material and the physical and the biological. Some would call a halt to the law, that all life must nourish itself, and assert that the soul can find its satisfying food here below without any appeal to a higher life. But the broken minds and tortured hearts testify to the fact that nothing can satisfy the soul hunger of man, except a nourishment suited to his soul and its aspirations for the perfect. A canary does not consume the same kind of food as a boa constrictor, because its nature is different. Man's soul being spiritual demands a spiritual food. In the order of grace, this divine food is the Eucharist, or the communion of man with Christ and Christ with man.

This is not something contrary to the natural law, for if the chemical could speak, it would say to the plant: "Unless you eat me, you shall not have life in you." If the plant could speak, it would say to the animal: "Unless you eat me, you shall not have life in you." If the animal, plant, and air could speak, they would say to man: "Unless you eat me, you shall not have life in you." With the same logic, but speaking from above and now below, because the soul is spiritual, Our Blessed Lord actually says to the soul: "Except you eat the Flesh of the Son of Man and drink His Blood, you shall not have life in you." The law of transformation works consistently through nature and grace. The lower transforms itself into the higher, the plant transforms itself into the animal when taken as food; man is transformed by grace into Christ when he takes Christ into his soul, for it is a quality of love to transform itself into the object that is loved.

Why should we be surprised that He gives Himself to us as food? After all, if He furnishes food for the birds and the beasts in the natural order, why should He not furnish it for man in the supernatural order? If the plant nourishes its seed before it is ripe, and if the bird brings food to its young before they can fly, shall we deny to Him that which we allow to a creature? To every infant at the breast, the mother virtually says: "Take, eat and drink; this is my body and blood." The mother would be untrue to nature if she said, "This *represents* my body," knowing that it *is* her body. So too, the Lord would be untrue to fact if He said: "This is not My Body and Blood. It is only a representation or a symbol of it." The analogy with the mother, however, breaks completely down, because here a nourishment is on the same level, that of the human with the human. But in the Eucharist, the nourishment is on two different levels: The divine and the human.

Union with the Life of Christ

If Christianity were only the memory of someone who lived over nineteen hundred years ago, it would not be worth preserving. If He Who came to this earth is not God, as well as Man, then we are dealing merely with the fallible and the human. But even granting that He is God in the flesh, how do we contact Him? Certainly, not by reading books about Him, although they are edifying and instructive; obviously not by singing hymns, though these do help us emotionally. The human heart craves contact with the beloved. If we can have contact with nature through the food we eat; if lower creation winds up somehow inside of my body, why should not means be provided in order that there might be communion of the soul? This is one of the first effects of Holy Communion: we receive from Christ what we gave to Him. We gave to him our human nature—when, in the name of all humanity, Mary gave Him manhood, like unto us in all things save sin. He divinized that human nature because it was made substantially one with His Divine Person. In Communion, He gives it back to us, purified, regenerated, ennobled, a promise and a pledge of what our nature is to be on the Last Day in the resurrection of the just. Our Blessed Lord made it so clear, it is almost difficult to understand how one misses it:

> As I live because of the Father, the Living Father who has sent me, so he who eats me will live, in his turn, because of me.
> (JOHN 6:58)

> . . . That they may all be one; that they too may be one in us, as thou Father, art in me, and I in thee; so that the world may come to believe that it is thou who has sent me. And I have given them the privilege which thou gavest to me, that they should all be one as we are one. (JOHN 17:21, 22)

In the natural order, a living thing assimilates its food and incorporates it into its own substance. In the Eucharist, the roles are reversed. The Eucharist is food for our soul, but the power of assimilation here belongs to Christ, and it is He Who, feeding us, unites us and incorporates us with His life. It is not Christ Who is changed into us, as is the food we eat; it is we who are incorporated in Him. With John the Baptist we say: "He must become more and more; I must become less and less."

The moment of communion is that special intimacy reserved to real lovers. There are three intimacies in life: hearing, speaking, and touching. Our first contact with anyone who loves us is to hear his voice, our second is to see him, the third—and this is reserved only for intimates—is the privilege of touch. We *hear* of Christ in the Scriptures, we *see* Him by the eyes of faith, but we *touch* Him in the Eucharist. He only asks that we should purge our consciences of sin and come to Him, ready to receive what He wants to give us for He knows that we need Him.

Second Effect: Union with the Death of Christ

Holy Communion is incorporation not only to the life of Christ, but also to His death. This second aspect is sometimes forgotten. St. Paul mentions it: "So it is the Lord's death that you are heralding, whenever you eat this bread and drink this cup, until he comes" (I CORINTH. 11:26). In another place, St. Paul tells us that we are to fill up in our own body that which is wanting to the Passion of Christ. To save our souls, the life of Christ must be duplicated in our own life. What He did in His birth, at Calvary, in His Resurrection, and Ascension, we must do. But we cannot enter into those heavenly blessings except through the touch of the Cross, namely, through penance, mortification, and self-denial, and a death to our egotism.

Hence, the Church insists that we be in the state of grace in order to receive Our Lord in the Eucharist. As a corpse cannot receive nourishment, so neither may one without the divine life in his soul receive the divine nourishment. In addition to this, the Church demands a certain amount of fasting before Communion. This is to remind us that the Eucharist is not only a sacrament of life, but also the sacrament of mortification. Only when we are stamped with the sign of the Cross will we be stamped with the glory of His Resurrection. From the moment of His death on Calvary until the end of time when He comes in glory, the dying Christ is continually at work representing His death on the altar, and urging us to represent it in our detachment from the seven pallbearers of the soul—the seven capital sins.

64

We are the wax and He is the seal. He wants to see something of His victimhood in us; and it is up to every Christian, therefore, to lead a dying life: to be more humble when we are thwarted, more patient when things go wrong, dying a little to the world and to our selfishness, being ever happy to "herald His death in our body until He comes."

Third Effect: Communion with the Mystical Body of Christ

No one was ever so wrong as the professor who said: "Religion is what a man does with his solitariness." If man is solitary, he is like a cell that is isolated from the body. The body can live without an individual cell, but the cell cannot live without the body. No man can live the divine life without some incorporation either in fact, or in desire, with the Mystical Body of Christ which is the Church. But the Mystical Body of Christ can live without an individual member. Our Blessed Lord described our union with Himself the night He gave the Eucharist, as that of the "vine and the branches." St. Paul speaks of us, too, as being many and yet one because we all eat the one bread. There is no autonomic individualism in the Scriptures or in humanity. The whole historical existence is transformed; that is to say, both humanity and the visible creation. The first was transformed through the Incarnation; the second, through the sacraments and its symbols which animate personality.

As there is a lymph which passes through the human body, each cell drinking of that life; so too, the Eucharist is the Divine lymph of the Mystical Body of Christ on which every member feeds. The members of the Church are not little spiritual islands each cherishing its own isolation. What blood plasma is to the physical body, the Eucharist is to the Mystical Body—the bond of its unity: "The one bread makes us one body, though we are many in number" (I CORINTH. 10:17).

The Tabernacle

The Blessed Sacrament is present in the Tabernacle day and night. There Christ dwells, body, blood, soul, and divinity, under the sacramental appearances of bread. How do we know it? Because Christ told us so! Is there any other fundamental evidence? None other than that; but is there any other reason in the world as strong as the word of God Himself? Hence, the Eucharist is above all other sacraments—it is the sacrament of faith.

The faithful believe that Christ is as really and truly present sacramentally in the Tabernacle as you are present while you read this book. It is this that makes the Church different from any other building. Not a pulpit, not an organ, not a choir, but Christ is the center. As the tabernacle was the center of worship in the Old Testament, so the tabernacle and the altar are the center of worship in the New Testament. Visitors to the Church say they "feel the difference," though they know nothing about the Eucharist, as they might feel heat and know not the nature of fire.

But to the faithful members of Christ's Mystical Body, here is Christ! Before His Eucharistic presence, the downcast eyes of sin find wealth of purging tears; here the heart wounded by betraying loves breaks its silence to the invitation of the Living Savior: "Child, give Me thy heart." Here the knee is humbled in genuflection and the heart exalted in adoration; here priests make their "Holy Hour" in answer to the invitation of their Lord in the Garden. Here is the trysting place of love, for this is the "bread which is come down from heaven" (JOHN 6:41–2) and will remain with us "unto the consummation of the world" (MATT. 28:20). Here Emmaus lives again as His disciples recognize Him in the breaking of the bread.

IV

THE SACRAMENT
OF PENANCE

The Sacrament of Penance is for spiritual wounds received after Baptism. Original sin was washed from the infant in Baptism, and in the case of the adult, personal sins as well. But the Lord is "practical." He knows that the white robe given in Baptism is not always kept immaculate; that the "just man falleth seven times a day," and that the offenses against us should be forgiven "seventy times seven." Therefore, in His mercy, He instituted a sacrament which is a tribunal of mercy for spiritual healing.

There have been those who say that there is no difference between the Sacrament of Penance and psychoanalysis because, in both, the human mind, when disturbed, seeks to throw off its burden. True it is that as the hand will go to the eye to provide relief from a speck, so the tongue will come to the aid of the heart to secure relief. As Shakespeare put it: "My tongue will tell the anger of my heart; Or else my heart, concealing it, will break." We are not here criticizing the psychoanalytic method, but only the error of saying that there is no difference between it and the Sacrament of Penance. But the differences between psychoanalysis and confession are enormous.

Contrast of Psychoanalysis and Confession

Psychoanalysis is the avowal of an attitude of *mind;* confession is an avowal of *guilt.* The first comes from the subconsciousness, the other from conscience. A person can be proud of his state of mind; some are proud of being atheists, or immoral, or gangsters. Many a patient will tell a psychiatrist, "Have you ever heard a case like mine, Doctor?" On the contrary, no one is ever proud of his guilt. Even in isolation, the sinner is ashamed. It takes no courage to admit that one is "mental" but guiltless; but it takes a tremendous amount of heroism, of which few are capable, to take the burden of one's own guilt to Calvary and lay one's hands at the feet of the Crucified and say: "I am responsible for this."

Psychoanalysis proceeds according to a *theory,* and not always one theory. Confession, however, is based upon conformity or non-conformity to the absolute standard of the *law of God.* Psychoanalysis does not agree on a particular theory by which a mental state is to be judged. There are three main theories: one attributes mental disturbances to sex (Freud); another to an inferiority complex (Adler); and the third to a drive toward security (Jung). The analyst, because he is guided by a theory, is *never required to have any moral fitness for his task;* his personal ethical right to receive confidences is never raised. He may be living with his sixth wife, and yet advise people how to be happy in marriage.

But in confession, it is different. The deliverances of the penitent are always on the *moral* plane—not on the *psychological.* The penitent knows that he is before a judgment, not a theory, and that the confessor who hears his sins stands in the place of God. Because the priest is the mediator between God and man, the Church always asks that the priest who absolves the penitent be himself in the state of grace; that is to say, a participant in divine life. The avowal of guilt, therefore, on the part of the penitent is not subject to the individual whims, theories, idiosyncrasies, and kinks of the one who hears it, but to the divine law, and to the order and the moral standards of Christ Who taught that one must be holy to make holy.

A third difference is that in psychoanalysis, there is the probing by an alien or *outside* mind; in confession, it is the *penitent himself* who is his own prosecuting attorney and even his own judge. In analysis, there is often a seeking out of attitudes to bolster up a theory; but in a spontaneous confession, the penitent analyzes his own faults and confesses them without having them wander and riot in "free association" and then be submitted to "private interpretation of the subconscious" which took the place of private interpretation of the Bible. Man naturally accords pardon to others who have done injury by a simple avowal of faults, without someone else dragging them out. One indispensable condition of receiving pardon in the sacrament is this *open* avowal of guilt, such as the prodigal son made when he returned again to the father's house.

Another difference is that what is told in the confessional is absolutely secret, and may never be divulged, or made part of a book, or turned into a case history, such as is often done with the material that is brought out in a psychoanalytic examination. The offenses man commits against God *do not belong to any man;* hence, he may not make use of them. The material of confession belongs to God, and sins may never be revealed by the confessor until God does so on the Day of Judgment. The confessor's ears are God's ears, and his tongue may never speak what God has heard through his ears.

Another difference is in the attitude that a person assumes in confession and psychoanalysis. In one instance, the mentally disturbed person is on a *couch;* in confession, he is on his *knees.* There is a passivity about the admission of a mental state on a couch; but there is a humble activity on the part of one who admits moral guilt while on his knees. In the psychological examination, there is never any such thing as contrition or satisfaction. In confession, sorrow and the making up for our sins are integral parts of the sacrament. When one sees a string of confessional boxes in a large church, with feet protruding from under the curtains like wiggling worms, one realizes that man has reduced himself almost to the humble state of the worm, in order that he might rise again, restored to the glorious friendship of the Christ Who died for him.

A final and important difference between psychoanalysis and confession is this: in psychoanalysis, the admission of mental states comes from ourselves; in confession, the impetus or the desire to confess our sins is from the *Holy Spirit.* The night of the Last Supper, Our Blessed Lord said that He would send His Spirit to convict the world of sin (JOHN 16:8). It is only through the Spirit of Christ that we know we are sinners, as we see our lives in relationship to the Cross. The Holy Spirit summons the soul to find its way back to the shelter of the Father's arms. When a person is in sin, he is in exile from home, a dweller in a foreign land who looks forward to the joy of return. It is an urge to share in the joy of the Good Shepherd as he carries back the lost sheep and the straying lamb to the sheepfold of the Church.

The reason this summons must come from God is that we are captives of sin. Just as a prisoner cannot release himself from the chafing bars or chains, so neither can the sinner without the power of the Spirit. To God alone belongs the initiative in this sacrament. It is His voice which calls us to repentance. We may make our confessions because our conscience urges us to do so, but the voice that speaks to us is the voice of the Holy Spirit telling us of God's mercy and love and righteousness. Under the impetus of the Holy Spirit, the soul feels like Lazarus risen from the dead.

Two Basic Requirements for the Sacrament

In order that there might be a Sacrament of Penance, two things are required, both of which are, from a human point of view, almost impossible to find. First, one must create the penitent and, secondly, one must create a confessor. To create a penitent, one must take a man in his pride, enveloped in a glacial silence, which refuses to unburden its guilt, and say to him: "Thou shalt come to a man and kneel before him—a man who is perhaps no better than you are—and you shall tell him what you hide from yourself and your children. You shall tell him that which makes you blush; and you shall do all of this on your knees."

However difficult it may be to create a penitent who will confess everything with a firm purpose of amendment, it is even more difficult to create the confessor. Where find one empowered by God with authority to forgive sins? How train the human heart to heal the wounds of others, and then seal his lips forever that what he has learned as God's representative be never revealed to men?

Only God could bring these two creations together, for outside of His power and mercy, we would say: "Humanity is too proud, you will never have penitents"; "Humanity is too indiscreet, you will never have confessors." And yet the sacrament exists. There are penitents because there are confessors, and there are penitents and confessors because Christ is God.

The Sacrament Deals with Sins

When a baby is born, it is generally healthy; but as time goes on, it becomes subject to diseases and organic troubles which oppress and torment life. In the spiritual order, too, though the soul is made clean and free from all sin by Baptism, it nevertheless contracts stains and spiritual diseases during life. These are known as sins. If the sin is serious enough to rupture the divine life within, then it is called "mortal" because it brings death to the life of Christ in the soul. If the wrong done does not destroy the divine life, but only injures it, it is called "venial."

A serious sin always produces in the soul a three-fold effect. The first is self-estrangement. A sinner feels in his inmost being like a battlefield

70

where a civil war rages. He no longer is a unit but a duality in which two forces within him struggle for mastery.

Serious sin estranges the sinner from his fellow man, because a man who is not at peace with himself will not be at peace with his neighbor. World wars are nothing but the projection, into great areas of the earth's surface, of the psychic wars waging inside of muddled souls. If there were no battles going on inside of hearts, there would be no battlefields in the world. It was after Cain's murder of Abel that he asked the anti-social question, "Am I my brother's keeper?"

The most serious effect of sin is not alienation from self and from fellow man; it is the estrangement from God. Inasmuch as grace is the divine life within the soul, it follows that a serious sin is the destruction of that divine life. That is why the *Epistle to the Hebrews* asks: "Would they crucify the Son of God a second time, hold Him up to mockery a second time, for their own ends?" (HEB. 6:6) Sin, therefore, is a second death. The merits we gained are lost; but those merits can be regained, thanks to the mercy of God, in the Sacrament of Penance.

Instituted by Christ

The Sacrament of Penance was instituted by Christ in the form of a judgment, for the remission, through sacramental absolution, of sins committed after Baptism and granted to a contrite person confessing his sins.

All through the Old Testament there was a preparation for this sacrament, inasmuch as God strove to induce men to acknowledge their sins before Him. To elicit a confession, God said to Adam: "Hast thou eaten of the tree?" God said to the first murderer: "Where is thy brother?" In Mosaic legislation, a sinner brought a sin offering, which was burned in a public place, to show that the sinner was not afraid to admit his guilt. The prophet, Nathan, heard David's confession after his sin with Bethsabee, and assigned to him a penance. John the Baptist heard the confession of those who came to hear him preach. These were only types and figures of the sacrament that was to come, because forgiveness became possible only through the merits of Our Lord's Passion.

No one questions the fact that Our Blessed Lord had the power to forgive sins. The Gospels record the miraculous cure of the paralytic at Capharnaum. Our Lord first told the paralytic that his sins were forgiven him, whereupon those round about laughed at Him. In response the Savior told them that it was just as easy to cure the man as it was to forgive his sins; so He cured the paralytic: "To convince you that the Son of Man has authority to forgive sins while He is on earth" (Mark 2:10).

Our Blessed Lord was saying that God in the form of Man had the power to forgive sins; that is to say, through the instrumentality of the human nature, which He received from Mary, He was forgiving sins. Here is an anticipation of the fact that it is through humanity that He will continue to forgive sins; i.e., through those who are endowed with sacramental power to do so. Man cannot forgive sins, but God can forgive sins through man.

Our Lord promised to confer this power of forgiveness, first of all, to Peter whom He made the rock of the Church. He told Peter that He would ratify in heaven the decisions which Peter took on earth. These decisions were explained in two metaphors of "binding" and "loosing." The power of jurisdiction was given to the one who had the keys of the kingdom. This promise made to Peter was followed up a little later on by one made to the Apostles. The second promise did not bestow the primacy, for that was reserved to Peter. Our Lord told the Apostles:

> I came upon an errand from my Father, and now I am sending you out in my turn. With that, he breathed on them, and said to them, Receive the Holy Spirit; when you forgive men's sins, they are forgiven, when you hold them bound, they are held bound.
> (John 20:21-23)

Our Divine Redeemer here says that He was sent by the Father; now He sends them with the power to forgive or not forgive. These words imply "hearing confessions," because how would the priests of the Church know which sins to forgive and which sins not to forgive if they did not hear them?

One can be very sure that this sacrament is not of human institution, for if the Church had invented any of the sacraments, there is one that it certainly would have done away with, and that is the Sacrament of Penance. This because of the trials that it imposes upon those who have to hear confessions, sitting in the confessional box for long hours while listening to the terrific monotony of fallen human nature. Because it is a divine institution—what a beautiful opportunity it is to restore peace to sinners and to make them saints!

It may be asked, why did Our Lord demand a telling of sins? Why not bury one's head in one's handkerchief, and tell God that one is sorry? Well, if this method of being sorry is not effective when we are caught by a traffic policeman, why should it be effective with God? Shedding tears in one's handkerchief is no test of sorrow, because we are then the judges.

Who would ever be sentenced to prison, if every man were his own judge? How easy it would be for murderers and thieves to escape justice and judgment simply by having a handkerchief ready!

Because sin is pride, it demands a humiliation, and there is no greater humiliation than unburdening one's soul to a fellow man. Such self-revelation cures us of many a moral illness. Hurtful things often hurt more if they are shut up. A boil can be cured, if lanced to release the pus; so too is a soul on the pathway to the Father's House when it admits to its own sin and seeks forgiveness. All nature suggests an unburdening of oneself. If the stomach takes a foreign substance into it which it cannot assimilate, it throws it off; so it is with the soul. It seeks deliverance from that which troubles it, namely the unbearable repartee within.

Furthermore, when a sin is avowed and admitted, it loses its tenacity. Sin is seen in all its horror when viewed in relationship to the Crucifixion. Suppress a sin, and it becomes buried, and later on will come out in complexes. It is very much like keeping the cap on a tube of toothpaste. If one submits it to great pressure, the toothpaste will come out somewhere; one does not know where. The normal place for it to come out is through the top. So too, if we suppress our guilt or deny it, we put our mind under pressure and it creates abnormalities. The guilt does not come out where it ought to be, namely, in the sacrament. Thus it was that Lady Macbeth's guilt came out in the washing of hands. It should have been her soul that was washed, and not her hands.

Confession to a Priest

It may be asked, why confess one's sins to a priest? Maybe he is not as holy as the penitent. That indeed could be. But though he is not holier in his *person,* he is holier in his *powers,* because Christ gave this power to His Church—only the Church claims it, and only the Church exercises it. The mayor of a town may not be as good as some of the citizens, but he has the power which the citizens do not; so it is with the priest.

Furthermore, it is not the priest who absolves: he is only the instrument of Christ. Can man of and by himself forgive sins? No! Can man united to God forgive sins? Yes! That is the way Christ the Son of God forgave sins through His human nature. That is the way He forgave the sins of Magdalen; that was the way He forgave the sins of the paralytic, that was the way He forgave the sins of the thief on the right. That power He gave to His Church.

Because the priest acts in Christ's name, he is bound by the seal of confession. Not even under the penalty of death may he reveal sins that

74

are confided to him in confession. As a person, he has not heard any sins. They are not a part of his knowledge. It was Christ Who heard the sin and He alone has knowledge of it. Suppose a murderer came into a rectory and confessed to a priest. On leaving the priest, the murderer shook hands with him. After the murderer left, the police entered, found blood on the priests's hands and accused him of the murder. The priest could not say: "It was the man who just went out. I did not do it." He may not make any defense of himself, nor may a priest outside the confessional ever speak to that person about his sins. For example, he may not say to a penitent whom he meets on the street, "Oh, did you ever pay back the hundred dollars you stole?" If someone stole money from a drawer in my desk, and then came and confessed the stealing of money; I could order the money returned, but I would not be permitted to lock the drawer, because that was information which I gained in God's sacrament.

Another reason for confessing sins to a priest is that no one sin is individual. We are members of the Mystical Body of Christ. If one member is unhealthy, the whole body is unhealthy. If we have an earache, the whole body suffers. Now, every personal sin has a social effect: all the other cells of the body of the Church are affected because of the defect in this one cell. Every sinner is blameworthy, not only in regard to himself, but also in regard to the Church, and first and foremost to God. If he is ever to recover, it can only be by the intervention of the Church, and by an intervention of God.

No medicine will act on a member of the body, unless the body co-operates in some way with the medicine. Because every sin is against God and the Church, it follows that a representative of God and His Mystical Body must restore the sinner again to fellowship. The priest, acting as the representative of the Church, welcomes back the penitent to the community of believers. When Our Blessed Lord found the lost sheep, He immediately integrated them again into His flock:

> "Jesus was to die for the sake of the nation; and not only for that nation's sake, but so as to bring together into one all God's children, scattered far and wide."   (JOHN 11:52)

The priest re-establishes the sinner in grace; he restores the sinner to his rights as a son of the Eternal Father; he reconciles him not only to God, but also to God's society of the Church.

The social nature of Penance is seen further in the fact that the penitent recognizes the right of the Mystical Body to judge him, since it is through the Mystical Body he is in relation with God. Forgiveness of sin, then, is not just a matter between God and our individual souls. It is the Church which has been injured by transgressions. Therefore, our sins are not just our concern, they are the concern of the whole Church—the Church Militant on earth and the Church Triumphant in heaven.

The Examination of Conscience

Before the penitent goes into the confessional box, there is the examination of conscience. This used to be a daily practice of Christians, and still is among many. It was not even unknown to the pagans. The Stoics, for example, recommended it. The examination of conscience centers not only on the wrong we have done, but also on the motivations. Our Blessed Lord, examining the conscience of the Pharisees, called them "whited sepulchres, clean on the outside, but on the inside full of dead men's bones." He pierced beneath the pretensions and hypocrisies of their prayers, their almsgivings, and their philanthropies, saying they did these things to be seen by men and to have a human reward—and that is the only reward they will ever receive. So in the examination of conscience, all the thoughts, words, and deeds of the soul are brought to the surface, examined, and considered in conformity with the law of God.

One of the differences between psychoanalytic examination and examination of conscience is that in the former one stands in one's own light; in the examination of conscience, one stands in the light of God. That is why Scripture says, "Search my soul, O my God." The divine light looks into the mind, takes the mind off itself and its own false judgments, and makes things appear as they really are; at the end, one does not say, "Oh, what a fool I've been," but rather, "God, be merciful to me, a sinner."

A day comes when the abused conscience will turn with fury and harass its victim, tormenting his waking life and making his dreams a poison and his darkness a nightmare. When night gives inner vision scope, the guilty conscience lies awake fearful of being known in its ugliness. There is nothing that so much arouses an unhealthy fear as a hidden guilt. As the cock crowed when Peter denied Our Lord, so our nature rises in revolt against us when we have denied the Lord of conscience. Sins have a way of finding us out. Just as a refusal to study in childhood begets an ignorance in mature life, so too, sins which we rationalize away are thrust down into unconsciousness, but somehow they make themselves felt in our health, our mental attitudes and our general outlook on life.

Alongside every human being there are three pools, each of which gives a different reflection. We look into one pool and we are pleased with ourselves, because in that pool we see ourselves as we think we are. In the second pool, we see ourselves as our neighbor sees us, or as our press

76

PRAYER BEFORE THE EXAMINATION OF CONSCIENCE

O most m̲e̲r̲c̲i̲f̲u̲l̲ G̲o̲d̲, I
thank Thee fo̲r̲ ̲T̲h̲y̲ ̲m̲e̲r̲c̲y̲
unto me, and ̲f̲o̲r̲ ̲s̲p̲a̲r̲i̲n̲g̲ ̲m̲e̲
this time for T̲h̲y̲ ̲g̲o̲o̲d̲n̲e̲s̲s̲
and long sufferi̲n̲g̲,
notwith̲s̲t̲a̲n̲d̲i̲n̲g̲ my
grievous ̲s̲i̲n̲s̲;̲ ̲a̲n̲d̲ ̲o̲f̲ ̲T̲h̲y̲
great mer̲c̲y̲ ̲I̲ ̲m̲i̲g̲h̲t̲ ̲h̲a̲v̲e̲
fallen into ̲h̲e̲l̲l̲ ̲d̲e̲e̲p̲e̲r̲
than those wh̲i̲c̲h̲ ̲h̲a̲v̲e̲ ̲c̲o̲m̲-
mitted, and tha̲t̲ ̲I̲ ̲m̲i̲g̲h̲t̲ ̲h̲a̲v̲e̲
been cut off and cas̲t̲ ̲o̲u̲t̲.
O my God, althoug̲h̲ ̲I̲ ̲h̲a̲v̲e̲
been so ungrateful to ̲T̲h̲e̲e̲ ̲i̲n̲

times past, yet now I beseech
Thee to accept me, returning
to Thee with an earnest desire
to repent and devote myself to
Thee, my Lord and my God.

Receive my confession, and
spare me, O most gracious
L̲o̲r̲d̲. Rebuke me not in Thy
a̲n̲g̲e̲r̲,̲ ̲a̲n̲d̲ cast me not away
f̲r̲o̲m̲ ̲T̲h̲y̲ ̲f̲a̲ce, O good Jesus,
f̲o̲r̲ ̲T̲h̲o̲u̲ ̲k̲n̲o̲w̲est Thou willest
n̲o̲t̲ ̲t̲h̲e̲ ̲d̲e̲a̲t̲h̲ ̲o̲f̲ a sinner, but
r̲a̲t̲h̲e̲r̲ ̲t̲h̲a̲t̲ ̲h̲e̲ ̲s̲h̲o̲uld be con-
v̲e̲r̲t̲e̲d̲.̲ ̲F̲o̲r̲g̲ive me, I
b̲e̲s̲e̲e̲c̲h̲ ̲T̲h̲e̲e̲,̲ ̲a̲m̲ing to
T̲h̲e̲e̲,̲ ̲a̲n̲d̲ ̲g̲r̲a̲n̲t̲ ̲a con-
f̲e̲s̲s̲i̲o̲n̲ ̲o̲f̲ ̲a̲l̲l̲ ̲m̲y̲ ̲most
g̲r̲i̲e̲v̲o̲u̲s̲ ̲s̲i̲n̲s̲,̲ upon
w̲h̲i̲c̲h̲ ̲I̲ ̲d̲o̲ ̲d̲e̲test

clippings reveal us. In the third pool, we see ourselves as God sees us, and as we *really* are. It is into this third pool that examination of conscience takes us, bringing to the surface the hidden faults of the day, discovering the weeds that are choking the growth of God's grace, our sins of omission and commission, the good deeds left undone, the failure to aid a needy neighbor, the refusal to offer a word of consolation to one burdened with sorrow, and malicious remarks, lies, acts of dishonesty, and the seven sins which are the enemy of peace: self-love, inordinate love of money, illicit sex, hate, over-indulgence, jealousy, and laziness.

Examination of conscience also embraces what is called our predominant passion. Every person has one sin which he commits more than another. Examination of conscience roots out all our self-deception, for every person has a little corner in his heart he never wants anyone to venture into, even with a candle. We say we are following our consciences, when actually what we mean is that we are making our consciences, and then following what we made. It is this kind of deceit that is unveiled in the examination and, by curing us of self-deception, it cures us of depression. Depression comes not from having faults, but from refusing to face them. What else is self-pity but a total unconcern with the interests of others?

It must not be thought that in the examination of conscience one concentrates on his own wounds; rather he concentrates on the mercy of God. A sick person thinks less of his own sickness than the physician who will heal him. The examination of conscience develops no complex, because it is done in the light of God's justice. The self is not the standard, nor is it the source of hope. All human frailty and human weakness are seen in the light of God's infinite goodness. Sorrow is aroused, not because a code has been violated, but because love has been wounded. As an empty pantry drives the housewife to the bakery, so the empty soul is driven to the bread of life. Examination of conscience, instead of inducing morbidity, becomes an occasion of joy.

There are two ways of knowing how good God is: one is never to lose Him through the preservation of innocence; the other is to find Him again after He has been lost. There is no self-loathing, there is only a God-loving character about the examination of conscience. We put ourselves in God's hand as we would put a broken watch in the hand of a watch maker, certain that he will not ruin it, but will make it function well.

The closer we get to God, the more we see our defects. A painting reveals few defects under candlelight, but the sunlight may reveal it as a daub. It is true that we do find ourselves quite unlovable in the examination of conscience, but it is this that makes us want to love God because He is the only One Who loves the unlovable.

78

When one has finished the examination of conscience, there may be a load to drag into the confessional, which is sometimes called the "box." If it is a "box," it is not Pandora's for at the bottom of it is hope. Then we realize that we are bringing it to Christ Himself. It is wonderful to know that there is one place where we can taste the freedom of heaven, where a man can be spared the hypocrisy of maintaining a pose. There comes the joy of knowing that neither the penitent nor the priest ever recalls the sin confessed. A shutter drops. Something is put into a well, and a cover is laid on it forever.

In the early Church, sins which were committed publicly were confessed publicly. This survives in the *Roman Pontifical*, in a ceremony called "The Expulsion of Public Penitents on Ash Wednesday"; another ceremony is called, "The Reconciliation of Penitents on Maundy Thursday"; and still another special rite is used for the absolution of those who have been publicly excommunicated. Though public sins in the early Church were confessed publicly, secret sins were confessed secretly and under the seal.

Sorrow for Sin: Contrition

The other sacraments demand that the subject has proper dispositions, but they do not constitute the *matter* of the sacrament. In Penance, sorrow is not only a condition, it is the *matter* itself; for without the sorrow for sin, forgiveness is not granted.

The priest gives absolution from sins in the sacrament provided there is sufficient sorrow of mind, or contrition, which is a hatred of the sin committed with the resolution not to sin again. The word contrition is taken from the Latin word which means to *grind* or *pulverize;* in an applied sense, it means being bruised in heart. Contrition is a sorrow of *mind,* not an emotional outburst or psychological remorse.

The prodigal son had gone through many emotional stages of remorse, particularly when he was feeding the swine, or realizing how much better the servants in his father's house were. But the real sorrow did not come until it penetrated his soul with the resolution: "I will arise and go to my father."

Sometimes it is said that all a Catholic has to do is go to Confession and admit his sins, and he will come out white as snow and then continue committing the same sins. This is a libel upon the sacrament for, where there is no purpose of amendment, there is no sorrow. The sins of such a penitent are *not* forgiven. The sorrow for sin necessarily includes a resolution not to sin again; this is not merely a wish which has no relationship to practice. Part of the act of contrition contains this amendment: "And I

80

firmly resolve with the help of Thy grace to confess my sins, to do penance, and amend my life. Amen." It means that here and *now* we take the resolution not to sin; we resolve to take all the *means* necessary for avoiding sin in the future, such as prayer and staying away from the occasions of sin. The absolution will not be efficacious if there is not in the sorrow this essential element, a purpose of amendment.

This does not imply an absolute certitude that no one will ever sin again, for that would be presumption. There are two ways to verify a firm purpose: one is to make up for the sin as soon as possible; for example, if one is guilty of sarcastic remarks against a neighbor, to seek the neighbor's pardon or, if one has stolen, to return what has been stolen. The second is to avoid the occasions of sin, such as bad reading, evil companions, drinking parties, or any act that previously led us into sin.

There are two kinds of contrition: perfect and imperfect. Both are implied in the Act of Contrition which the penitent says in the confessional:

> "And I detest all my sins because I dread the loss of Heaven and the pains of Hell," [imperfect sorrow]; "but most of all because they offend Thee, my God, Who art all good and deserving of all my love" [perfect sorrow].

Two kinds of fear serve as the basis of distinction between the two kinds of contrition or sorrow: one is a *servile* fear, the other is a *filial* fear. A *servile* fear is a fear of punishment, which we justly deserve from a master whom we disobeyed. *Filial* fear is the fear that a devoted son might have for a loving father; namely, the fear of injuring him. Applying this to contrition, servile fear draws us toward God because of the dread of a punishment for sin, namely, hell. *Filial* fear is a dread of being separated from God, or of offending Him Whom we love.

Imagine twins who had disobeyed a mother in exactly the same way. One of the twins runs to the mother and says: "Oh, Mommy, I am sorry I disobeyed. Now I can't go to the picnic, can I?" The other one throws her arms around the mother's neck and weeps: "I'll never hurt you again." The first has imperfect contrition, the second perfect contrition.

Which kind of contrition, perfect or imperfect, is sufficient in sacramental Confession? Imperfect contrition is sufficient, though it is our belief that most penitents are sorry not because of the punishment their sins deserve from God, but rather because they heartily are sorry for having recrucified Christ in their hearts.

Suppose, however, that a person is in a state of mortal sin and is unable to go to confession; for example, a soldier who is ordered into battle. Would

81

imperfect contrition then suffice for the forgiveness of sins? No, but perfect contrition would, if he had the resolution to receive sacramental confession at the earliest opportunity.

That makes a word about perfect contrition more imperative. The usual attitude of penitents is to make a personal equation between their own sins and the Crucifixion. Each one says in his heart as he receives the sacrament: "If I had been less proud, the crown of thorns would have been less piercing. If I had been less avaricious and greedy, His hands would have been dug less by the steel. If I had been less sensual, His flesh would not be hanging from Him like purple rags. If I had not wandered away like a lost sheep, in the perversity of my egotism, His feet would have been less riven with nails. I am sorry, not just because I broke a law: I am sorry because I wounded Him Who died out of love for me."

Our Lord had to die on the Cross before the abysmal dimensions of sin could be appreciated. We do not see the horror of sin in the crimes paraded in the press, nor in the great crises of history, nor in the wholesale violence of persecutors. We see what evil is only when we see *Goodness nailed to the Cross*. If any of us says in our heart, "I am not as bad as those who crucified Him," we are forgetting that *they* did not crucify Our Lord; sin did. They were our representatives, our ambassadors, that day at the court of Satan. We empowered them with the right to crucify.

One look at the crucifix, therefore, is a double revelation! A revelation of the horror of sin and the love of God. The worst thing that sin can do is not to kill children or bomb cities in nuclear warfare; the worst thing that sin can do is to crucify divine love. And the most beautiful thing that Love can do, at the moment of crucifixion, is to extend to us forgiveness in the priestly prayer to His heavenly Father: "Forgive them, for they know not what they do."

In perfect contrition, we become tremendously impressed with the infinite endurance of Our Lord to suffer the worst that evil can inflict, and then pardon his enemies. He certainly did not teach us to be indifferent to sin, because He took its full consequences upon Himself. He paid for it, but on the other hand, there was mercy with that justice. He offered forgiveness in the hope that we would repent out of gratitude for His payment of the debt which our sins created.

Satisfaction

Satisfaction for sins, or what is sometimes called "penance," is distinct from sorrow. Few dwell sufficiently on the difference between being forgiven and atoning for the sin which was forgiven.

Suppose I stole your purse in the course of a conversation, and then I said to myself: "What a scandal I am to this person. I am supposed to bring justice and the love of God, and here I violate God's law of justice, impugn His mercy, and nail Him to the Cross by stealing the purse." So I say to you, "Will you forgive me?" In your kindness, you would certainly say: "I forgive you." But you would also say something else, would you not? Would you not say, "Give me back my purse?" Could I really say that I was sorry unless I returned the purse?

There is a story told, which is sheer imagination with no basis in fact, about a man who came to confession to a priest. During the course of the confession, he stole the priest's watch. At the end of the confession, he said to the priest: "Oh, Father, I forgot to tell you. I stole a watch." The priest, emphasizing the necessity of satisfaction, said: "You must return the watch to the owner." The penitent said: "I'll give it to you, Father." The priest said: "No, I don't want it. Return it to the owner." The penitent said: "The owner doesn't want it." The priest said to him: "Well, in that case, you can keep it."

Immediately one can see some of the fallacies. First, there was no real sorrow in confession; otherwise, he would not have added a sin while confessing others. Second, there was deceit in his satisfaction. There must always be satisfaction for sin, because every sin disturbs the order of God. Sin upsets a balance. It is to no purpose to say, "Don't cry over spilled milk," just because we happen to have spilled someone else's milk. If we cannot gather up the spilled milk, we can at least pay for the bottle, or buy some more milk.

At the end of the confession, the priest gives to the penitent what is called a "penance," a certain number of prayers to say, or fasting, or the giving of alms, or acts of mortification, or a way of the Cross, or a rosary. All of these are to "make up" for the sin, and to prove that the sorrow was sincere. This is what Catholics call "saying my penance" or "doing my penance."

God does not ask us to make an exact reparation for our sins, but rather to do it in a proportional manner. This is because the Sacrament of Penance is less a tribunal of strict justice than a reconciliation between friends. The priest, representing Christ, is not a judge sentencing a criminal to prison. The penitent is not an enemy. He is a reconciled friend, and the reparation, penance, or satisfaction is the work of friendship between members of Christ's Mystical Body. The penance also has a medicinal value, that of healing the wounds of the soul, which is why it has to be performed in a state of grace. Our Lord forgave our sins on the Cross, but He paid for them in justice. Our Lord forgave the thief on the right, but He did not stop his crucifixion. The pain the thief endured was a reparation for his evil life. Penance is a sign that we are applying Christ's death on Calvary to ourselves.

Here the Sacrament of Penance differs from the Sacrament of Baptism. In Baptism, the merits of Christ's Passion are applied to ourselves without any action on our part; but in the Sacrament of Penance, we make some satisfaction. Power and efficacy are given to our acts, because they are united with the Passion of Christ. There are two debts to be paid for sin. One is the eternal debt, which is hell; and the other is the temporal debt, or atoning in our lifetime for our imperfections and our want of charity, after our sin has been forgiven. The *eternal* debt of hell is completely *remitted* in the sacrament. The *temporal* debt for sin remains.

In Scripture, we find records of people being forgiven, for whom a temporal punishment remains. Adam and Eve were restored to grace, but they were made subject to death. Miriam, the sister of Moses, gained forgiveness for her sin, but she was shut out from the camp for seven days and afflicted with leprosy. Moses was forgiven, but was punished for his lack of trust in God by being excluded from the Land of Promise. David's sin with Bethsabee was forgiven, but he had to suffer misfortunes for it, and the child died as a punishment.

That is why St. Paul urges us to take on voluntary penances that we may "help to pay off the debt which the afflictions of Christ still leave to be paid, for the sake of His Body, the Church." Daniel consoled Nabuchodonosor with the words: "Deign my lord king, to be advised by me; with almsgiving, with mercy to the poor, for fault and wrong-doing of thine, make amends; it may be that he will condone thy guilt" (DANIEL 4:24). And Joel writes: "Time now, the Lord says, to turn the whole bent of your hearts back to me, with fasting and mourners' tears" (JOEL 2:12). Did not Our Lord say of certain cities that they would be condemned because in them "were done most of His miracles, but for that they had not done penance" (MATT. 9:20).

Penances given after confession are generally light. Some say they are too light. But we must not forget indulgences. To understand them, we should recall that we are members of Christ's Mystical Body. When we do evil, or commit sin, we affect every member of the Church in some way. This is even done in our most secret sins. It is evident that we do it in stealing, murder, and adultery; but we do it even in our solitary sins, even in our evil thoughts. How? By diminishing in some way the content of charity and love within the whole Mystical Body. Just as a pain in the eye affects the whole organism and makes us hurt all over so, if I love Christ less, do I impair the spiritual well-being of the Church.

But because I can harm the Church by my sin, so can I be helped by the Church when I am in debt. St. Paul applied to the Mystical Body the lesson of the physical body: "All the different parts of it [the body] were to make each other's welfare their common care" (I CORINTH. 12:25).

Religion is not individual, it is *social;* it is organic. Look to the natural order, and see how many benefits I receive from my fellow man. There are a million ways in which they are indulgent to me. I did not raise the cow that furnished the leather that went into my shoes. I did not raise the chicken I eat at dinner—but that is a bad example; I do not like chicken! So let us say, the chicken you eat. Somebody's work or labor allowed you to indulge in this luxury. We might almost say that we are surrounded by social "indulgences," because we share in the merits, talents, arts, crafts, sciences, techniques, needlework, and genius of society.

Now, in the society of Christ's people, His Mystical Body, it is possible to share in the merits and the good works, the prayers, the sacrifices, the self-denials, and the martyrdoms of others. If there be an economic "indulgence," so that I can ride in a plane someone else built, why should there not also be a spiritual indulgence, so that I can be carried to Christ more quickly through the bounty of some members of the Mystical Body.

Go back now to the distinction between forgiveness of guilt and satisfaction for guilt. Every sin has either an eternal or a temporal punishment. Even though our sins were forgiven, there still remained some satisfaction to be made in time; or else in Purgatory after death, provided we die in the state of grace. An indulgence refers not to sin, but to the temporal punishment. Before the indulgences can apply, there must have been forgiveness of the guilt.

Actually, there are several ways of making up for the punishment due after the guilt of sin has been forgiven. Three are personal, one is social: (1) The saying or doing of the penance given in the confessional box at the end of confession; (2) Any works of mortification which are freely undertaken during life, such as helping the poor and the missions, fasting, and other acts of self-denial; (3) The patient imitation of Our Lord's sufferings on the Cross by enduring the trials of life; and (4) The social remedy of applying the superabundant merits of the Mystical Body to our souls. As we depend on intellectual society to make up for our ignorance, so we depend on a spiritual society to make up for our spiritual bankruptcy.

It may be asked where the Church gets power to remit temporal punishment due to sin? Well, the Church happens to be very rich *spiritually,* just as some men are very rich financially. In a village there lived a rich banker who set up a trust fund in a bank; he bade all of the sick, infirm, and unemployed to draw from that reserve. The banker told them: "Have no fears that this fund will ever run out, for I am rich enough to care for all of you." If the banker paid part of the hospital bills, that would be a *partial indulgence* of the debts of the sick; if he paid all of their bills, that would be a *plenary indulgence* of their expenses and costs.

The Church is a spiritual banker. It has all the merits of the Passion of Our Lord and the Blessed Mother, the merits of the martyrs, saints, and confessors, and the patient endurance of persecution in the present time; all of these merits are far greater than those needed for salvation of these saintly and good people. The Church takes that surplus, puts it into her treasury, and bids all her weak and wounded, who cannot pay all the debts they owe for their sins, to draw on those reserves. The Church lays down certain conditions for making use of this treasure, just as the banker did. The users have to be deserving, they have to be in the state of grace, they have to fulfill certain conditions; e.g., a prayer, a pilgrimage, or any one of a thousand little things.

When the debt of temporal punishment due to sin is liquidated only in part by an indulgence, it is called a *partial indulgence*. But if all the debts of temporal punishment are paid for by fulfilling the conditions, it is called a *plenary indulgence*.

Suppose I am standing in the center of the room, that you have a right to command me, and that I am bound in conscience to obey you. You order me to take three steps to my right. I disobey, and take three steps to my left. When I take the three steps to my left, I say to you, "I am very sorry. I have disobeyed you. Will you forgive me?" You say: "Yes, I will forgive you." But look where I am! I am actually six steps from where I ought to be, and I am three steps from being in neutral ground. Since I have taken three steps in disobedience, I must put my foot down three times humbly and in penance, in order to get back to "neutral" before I can begin doing right. Those three steps, taken penitentially, represent the payment of the temporal punishment due to sin.

Now suppose that I just took two steps and someone carried me the other one, I would then have an indulgence of one step. If someone carried me two steps, I would then have the indulgence of two steps. If someone carried me the three steps, that would be a plenary indulgence.

That brings up the question of "days." One often hears of the indulgence of "forty days," "one hundred days," or "forty years." The Church has to have some standard of measurement, and "days" and "years" are merely approximations. In the first several centuries of the Church, penances were very severe for certain public sins. One might have to dress himself in sackcloth and ashes and beg at a church door for forty days, or three years, or seven years, or sometimes ten years in the case of atrocious crimes.

Because these sins gave grave scandal to the public, the penitent would be permitted to assist at the Mass at the door or in a special part of the Church.

Later on, there began to be intercessions of persons of high merit, that they be given more or less extended remission of the temporal punishment due to their sins; these became known as indulgences. The Church then took, as a standard of measurement, the severe penances of the early days and applies them today to indulgences. For example, for saying certain prayers, one receives an indulgence which is the equivalent of "forty days" penance in the early Church, or the equivalent of "one hundred days" penance in the early Church, or a "year," as the case may be.

There is no exact statistical relation between the sin and its expiation, as there is none between the money you pay for a suit of clothes, and the cooperation of the sheep herder, the wool-gatherers, and the suit manufacturer.

What a beautiful doctrine and how consoling is this sacrament! See how it combines the poor sinner who is in debt, the Mystical Body to which he is restored by absolution in the confessional, and the mercy of Christ, the Head of His Mystical Body Who gave this power to His Church: "Whatsoever thou shalt loose on earth is loosed also in heaven."

My prayer is only a drop but, when it is joined to the other cells of the Mystical Body, when it becomes a bead in a rosary which unites the Church Militant on earth with the Church Triumphant in heaven and Church Suffering in purgatory, when it fuses into the tears of Christ on the Cross and with the sword in Mary's heart at the foot of the Cross, then it makes its way to the sea which is God where we all meet. Thus, thanks to my little drop of a prayer, I have the right to say, "I, too, am the ocean."

One feels like singing for joy, for here is a greater thrill than the bath that cleanses the body. Regular confession prevents sins, worries, and anxieties from seeping down into the unconscious and degenerating into melancholy fears and neuroses. The boil is lanced before the pus can spread into unconsciousness. Our Lord knew what was in man so He instituted this sacrament, not for His needs but for ours. It was His way of giving man a happy heart. It is not easy, indeed, for a man to make his way to the Cross and to admit that he has been wrong. It is very hard; but the penitent knows that it was harder to hang on that Cross! We are never made worse by admitting we are broken-hearted, for unless our hearts are broken, how can God get in?

V

THE SACRAMENT OF THE ANOINTING OF THE SICK

There are two sacraments of "healing": one for spiritual illness, which is the Sacrament of Penance; the other for physical illness, which is the Sacrament of the Anointing of the Sick. An older term for it was "Extreme Unction," which some interpreted as meaning that it was administered only when death was inevitable. For that reason, the sacrament was sometimes postponed until there was no hope of recovery, so as not to frighten the recipient or unduly sadden the relatives and friends.

This is a misinterpretation of the sacrament which is directed to the uncertainty which sickness implies; the sacrament looks to sickness as such. Two extremes are to be avoided, one which would say it was destined only for death; the other, that it is solely a grace of healing. It is rather a sacrament for the time of serious sickness; that is why it may not be given to those who are facing death for any reason other than illness. If it were a sacrament destined solely for those who are about to die, it would be given to a criminal on a scaffold. But the sacrament may not be given in such a case. It may be given immediately after electrocution or hanging, or any violent death, but not before. In those under sentence of death there is no hope of recovery, which this sacrament implies.

It is not a sacrament exclusively for those at the point of death. In the liturgy of the sacrament, the priest does not mention death, but prays for a return to health of body and soul:

> Heal, O Redeemer, the infirmities of the sick person; heal his wounds and forgive him his sins. Make all the infirmities of his body and soul disappear, and by Thy Mercy, give him full spiritual and corporal health, that re-established by the effect of Your goodness, he can resume the fulfillment of his duties. . . . Grant that Thy servant, freed from sickness and restored to health, may be re-established by Thy Name and given back to Thy Holy Church.

Two other prayers follow in which the restoration to health is emphasized:

> We implore Thee, O Lord, look with kindness on Thy servant [name] who is growing weak as his [her] body fails. Cherish and revive the soul which Thou didst create, so that, purified and made whole by his [her] sufferings, he [she] may find himself [herself] restored by Thy healing through Christ Our Lord. Amen.

> O Lord, Father Almighty, . . . free Thy servant from sickness. Restore to him [her] his [her] health. Raise him [her] up by Thy right hand, strengthen him [her] by Thy power, protect him [her] by Thy might, and give him [her] back to Thy Holy Church with all that is needed for his [her] welfare through Christ Our Lord. Amen.

The oil of the sick, which is consecrated at the Pontifical Mass on Holy Thursday, contains no allusions to death or the dying. The words of the bishop are:

> Pray that this oil may serve to give renewed strength to God's temple . . . that all who are anointed with the heavenly remedy of this oil may find it a medicine for body and soul, quick to remove all suffering and to drive away all sickness and infirmity of soul and body.

90

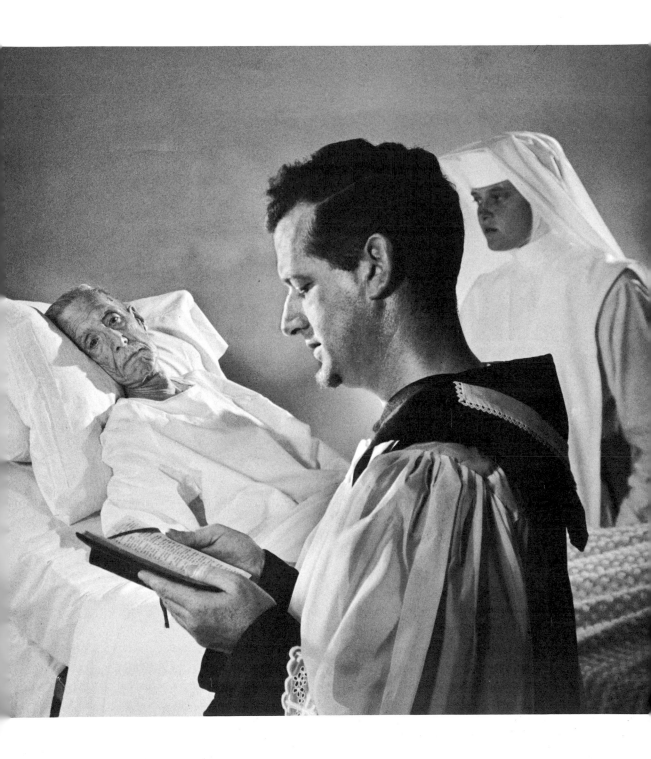

The official teaching of the Church condemns those who deny that it is a sacrament of healing. The Council of Trent stated:

> If anyone says that the anointing of the sick neither confers any grace nor remits sins, nor comforts the sick, but that it has already ceased, as if it had been a healing grace only in the olden days, let him be anathema.

When the salvation of the person, under providence, calls for the postponement of death, the sacrament will bring about this recovery. The writer recalls giving the Sacrament of the Anointing of the Sick to a woman who was given to a life of sin. She had been poisoned. As the poison infected the brain, she had the impression of losing each of the external senses. She would reach for her eye and say to her mother: "Mother, here is my eye. You keep it when I am gone." She would reach for her ear and say to me, "Here, you keep this when I am gone." The Sacrament of the Anointing of the Sick was administered and immediately she was restored to health. The next day she came to the rectory and began leading an apostolic life which continued for many years, until her death. The anointing was for her death, but it happened to be for a postponed death.

St. James, in describing the Sacrament of the Anointing of the Sick, puts the emphasis on the healing:

> Is one of you sick? Let him send for the presbyters of the church, and let them pray over him, anointing him with oil and the Lord's name. Prayer offered in faith will restore the sick man, and the Lord will give him relief; if he is guilty of sins, they will be pardoned.
>
> (JAMES 5:14, 15)

Here it is to be noted that the people who are to benefit are not necessarily those at death's door, but the sick. The sick man is described as one able to call in the priests of the Church. St. James says also that the prayer of faith shall save the sick man, which is the physical side of the sacrament; the forgiveness of sins being the spiritual side.

The purpose of the sacrament is clear from the fact that the *person* is sick—not the body alone, nor the soul alone. All the sacraments are aimed at a single whole, made up of matter and spirit. Even the Eucharist pertains to the body, as well as the soul, for Our Lord said that He would "raise up on the Last Day" those who would receive it. Sickness has spiritual reper-

92

cussions: no person can be sick in body without having his soul disturbed. The Anointing of the Sick, therefore, is to some extent *psychosomatic*.

Sickness and the Soul

A serious illness cuts us off from the occasion of sin. The will to sin is weakened by the physical inability to sin. It is true that many a man believes he has left the passions behind, when it is really that the passions have left him behind. This moment of enforced detachment from the allurements of the world is always an opportunity for the reception of grace.

The approach to death emphasizes the uniqueness of personality. During life we lose ourselves in the mob, in the anonymous "they," in the masses, in "togetherness." But the nearness of death confronts self with self: "I am I—unique—responsible for every thought, word, and deed of life." The soul begins to see itself as it really is, and God in His mercy prepares a sacrament for this dread moment when personality is confronted with its load of sin.

Sickness breaks the spell that pleasure is everything, or that we ought to go on building bigger and bigger barns, or that life is worthless unless it has a thrill. Sickness enables us to adjust our sense of values, as an actual grace illumines the futility and emptiness of many ambitions: "What does it profit a man if he gain the whole world and lose his soul?"

There is a world of difference between the Christian in serious illness and the pagan. As Franz Werfel wrote:

> The skeptic believes in nothing *more* than death; the believer
> believes in nothing *less*. Since the world to him is a creation of
> spirit and love, he cannot be threatened by eternal destruction
> in his essential being, as a creature of the world.

A man who in life never prepares for death, uses every means to conceal it, to render it unobtrusive, to disguise it, even feels awkward in the presence of death and knows not how to console those who are bereaved.

The pagan fears the loss of the body; the Christian fears the loss of the soul, knowing that the destiny of the body will be the destiny of the soul. To a pagan, this world is everything and death deprives him of all there is; to the Christian, this world is only a scaffolding through which souls climb to the Kingdom of God. When the last soul shall have climbed up through the scaffolding, then it shall be torn down and burned with fervent fire, not because it is base, but simply because it has done its work—it has brought us back again to God. Hence, to the Christian, his whole being is never threatened by death. All during life, the pagan is moving toward death; but the Christian is moving backward. He starts with the fact that he must die and render an account of his stewardship; knowing that he will die, he plans his life accordingly.

The Christian, having been signed with the sign of death, the sign of the Cross at Baptism, is committed to leading a life of mortification, which means a dying to the ego, in order that the Christ-life may be more manifest.

The Church is, therefore, constantly recommending a daily rehearsal for the great event, or tiny little deaths in preparation for the final one. No masterpiece is ever created in a day, and death itself is a masterpiece. The sculptor who wishes to carve a figure out of a block of marble uses his chisel; first cutting away great chunks of marble, then smaller pieces; finally he reaches a point where only a brush of the hand is needed to reveal the figure. In the same way, the soul at first has to undergo tremendous mortifications, then more refined detachments and little deaths until finally the divine image is revealed. Because mortification is recognized as a practice of death, it was fittingly described on the tomb of Duns Scotus: "*Bis mortuus; semel sepultus*"—He died twice, but was buried only once.

As evidence of how seriously the Church takes grace or divine life in the soul, in contrast to physical life, its liturgy calls the day on which saints die, their "birthday," or *natalitia.* The world celebrates a birthday on the day a person was born to physical life; the Church celebrates it when a person is born to eternal life. There are three exceptions to this in the liturgy of the Church, and for very good reasons. The only physical birthdays in the liturgy are those of Our Divine Lord (December 25th), the Blessed Mother (September 8th), and John the Baptist (June 24th). This is because each of these births marked a special infusion of divine life into the world: *Our Lord is Eternal Life;* the Blessed Mother, through her Immaculate Conception, participated in that eternal life from the first moment of her conception; and St. John the Baptist was sanctified in his mother's womb, when he was visited by his Lord, still tabernacled within the Blessed Mother.

This does not mean, even for the Christian, that death has no terrors. There is still something very frightening about it. If death were merely a physical *must,* we would not fear it; our fear comes from the moral fact that we know we ought not to die. We fear death because we realize it was not part of the original plan. The dying Christian knows that the personal

94

judgment at the moment of his death will be a revelation of the meaning of his personal life, just as the cosmic judgment at the end of time will be a revelation of how he lived in society.

Death is not just a mere emancipation of the soul from the limitations and burdens of the body, and a passage into a purely spiritual state, such as Plato conceived. This would completely forget the resurrection of the body. The body has had a share in the virtues or the vices of the soul; therefore, it will take on a quality after death corresponding to the quality of the soul. If a green liquid is poured into a glass, the glass looks green. If the liquid poured in is red, the glass looks red. So too, when evil is poured into the soul, the body takes on the quality of evil, and is in a state of incorruptible "corruption," whereas the body of the person who dies in the state of grace shares in the glory of the soul.

What this glorified body will be like we do not know, except that it will correspond with the "new heaven" and the "new earth" of which the *Apocalypse* speaks. When the soul leaves the body at death, it does not leave the body's sphere altogether. The soul still has a tendency to be reunited with the body. We put our hand on warm wax and we leave the imprint of the hand. So too, the imprint of the soul is in some way in the body, and the soul to some extent bears the body within itself. In the resurrection of the dead, God will give the soul its body-forming power, and the opportunity to build up the body will be entrusted to it, as it was meant to be.

To understand the sacrament, one must never lose hold of the fact that there is a double life: biological and spiritual. So there is a double death, death of body and death of the soul. St. John states: "Thou dost pass for a living man, and all the while art a corpse" (Apoc. 3:1). A body may be physically alive but the soul spiritually dead. Such would be a person in the state of serious sin and alienation from God. We see corpses walking on the street every day; biological life is in them, but not spiritual life.

The real reason man dies in his flesh is because his soul, having turned away from God, has lost the dominion it once exercised over the body. One of the penalties of original sin was that the body should die. When the sinful soul is restored to the state of grace, it has its power returned *potentially* to effect the quickening of the flesh and the restoration of the body, but the actual rejuvenation is deferred until the last day.

In its present state, the body often depresses the soul; it restrains it in its upward flight. It is almost a cage which prevents the soul, as a dove, from flying to God. A sickness accentuates this weight, producing some-

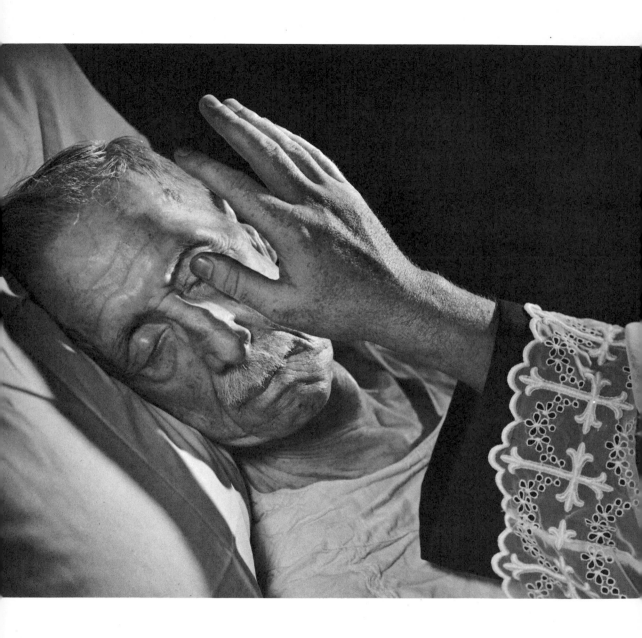

times a lethargy in the soul. Herein is the purpose of the Anointing of the Sick: to enable the soul to be free in this life, either through the healing of the body, or else to be eventually free from the body in death, with all the traces of sin blotted out.

How the Sacrament Is Administered

In speaking of the sacrament, St. James said that the priests of the Church were to be called in—not merely the priest. Though it is one person who is sick and one organism that is disordered, nevertheless, sickness is not considered a private affair any more than sin is a private affair. Just as one sin in a soul diminishes the sum or the content of charity in the Mystical Body, so the sickness of any one of the members of the Church, grieves in some way the fellowship of the saints. The Church, representing Our Lord, responds to this sickness in any one of her members, by sharing her own corporate wealth with the one who is ill. Her prayer is that the sick person be cured of his weakness, and if it be God's will, be restored to the life of the Mystical Body.

The unction of the sick is a kind of a prolongation both of Baptism and of Penance, in the sense that it is a remedy for sin. It is not to be thought that the sacrament operates in the sick in the nature of a miracle, or takes the place of medical science, any more than Baptism takes the place of birth, or Holy Communion takes the place of eating. The Council of Trent said that the Anointing of the Sick was a consummation not only of Penance, but of the whole Christian life which ought to be a continual penance. The Anointing of the Sick is a sacrament of the living and, therefore, normally presupposes the state of grace, just as medicine is given only to the living, and holy oil is a medicine.

As was pointed out above, physical life may have either wounds or diseases. There is a difference between having a finger cut by a knife and a body suffering from smallpox or cancer. Penance looks more to the wounds of the soul; Anointing of the Sick more to the sickness of the body, but never apart from the soul.

The administration of the sacrament starts with the basic psychological fact that we cannot think of a single sin that ever got into our soul that did not come through our body. The sin of envy, for example, comes through the eyes; we may have seen how much more the Joneses have. The sin of pride, in like manner, often comes from the eyes, as one makes a comparison between how much richer, smarter, or more beautiful one

97

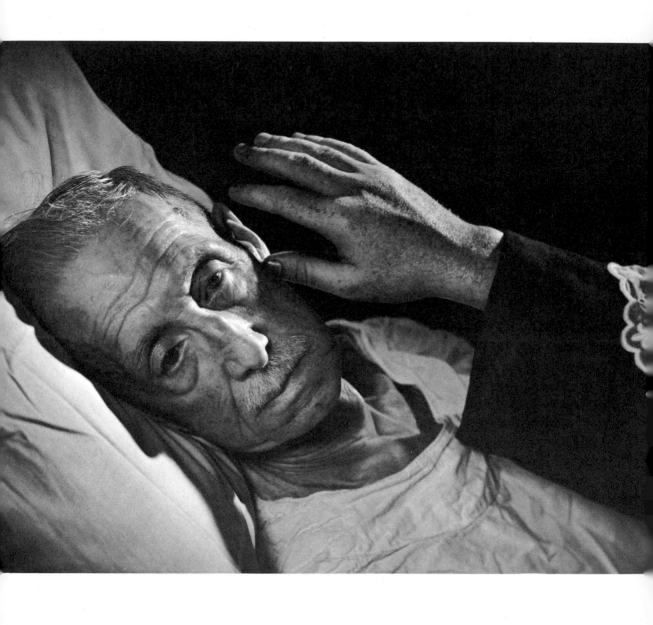

person is than another. Drunkenness, adultery, robbery, blasphemy—we often walk into these occasions of sin. Even the nose contributes to sin and to vanity, either through the smell of good food leading to gluttony, or through perfumes which, according to advertisements, are allurements to sin.

Just as physical diseases leave certain marks on the body—tuberculosis leaves spots on the lungs, smallpox marks on the face, leprosy scars—so too, sin leaves behind some traces in the senses and in the body. The spiritual scar of every sin is evident from the fact that one feels weaker after the sin than before, and less resistant to wrong. Other diseases or viruses leave little "tails"—not speaking scientifically—or traces of their existence in the body. Just as sewers become clogged and chimneys sooted and ships contract barnacles, so too, the germs of sin leave little "tails" behind, which are remnants or relics of the rebellion which ravished the soul and the body. Though an alcoholic may give up his alcohol and repent for his sin, alcoholism may remain in the body in marred and ruined organs.

The Church now comes along in a serious illness, not only to blot out the sin, which is done primarily in the Sacrament of Penance (also here if Penance cannot be received), but also to cleanse away the remains of sin. Because sin came into the soul through the eyes, ears and nostrils, mouth, hands and feet, the Church lays hold of these senses and organs which in some way cooperated with the soul in sinning. It prepares the soul either for the restoration to the Mystical Body of Christ or for a passage to God. The poor member of the Church is covered with the dust of action and the spatterings of life, with the mire and dregs of half-fought battles, with the weakness of swords half-drawn; with one eye toward the world and the other toward Christ. That is why the Church prays: "Remember not, then, his old sins, nor the excesses to which anger or the fervor of an evil will has led him. For, though he has sinned, yet he has not denied Thee, O God."

When the eyes are anointed, the priest says: "By this holy anointing and with His holy loving Mercy, may the Lord forgive you whatever wrong you may have done by the use of your sight. Amen."

When the ears are anointed, the priest says: "By this holy anointing and His most loving Mercy may the Lord forgive you whatever wrong you have done by the sense of hearing. Amen."

When the nose is anointed, the priest says: "By this holy anointing and His most loving Mercy, may the Lord forgive you whatever wrong you have done by your use of the sense of smell. Amen."

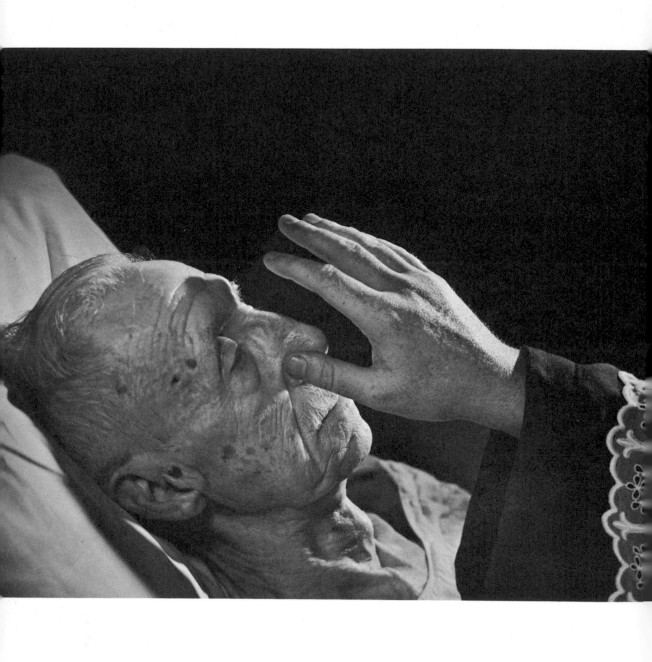

When the mouth with closed lips is anointed, the priest says: "By this holy anointing and His most loving Mercy, may the Lord forgive you whatever wrong you may have done by the use of the sense of taste and the power of speech. Amen."

When the hands are anointed, the priest says: "By this holy anointing and His most loving Mercy, may the Lord forgive you whatever wrong you may have done by the use of the sense of touch. Amen." The priest on dying is anointed on the back of his hands, his palms having been anointed in Holy Orders. The lay person is always anointed on the palms.

When the feet are anointed, the priest says: "By this holy anointing and His most loving Mercy, may the Lord forgive you whatever wrong you may have done by the use of your power of walking. Amen."

In the following prayer which the Church recites, there is no mention of death:

> Cure, we beseech Thee, our Redeemer, by the grace of the Holy Sacrament, the ailments of this sick man [woman]; heal his wounds and forgive his sins. Deliver him from all miseries of body and mind; mercifully restore him to perfect health inwardly and outwardly, that having recovered by an act of kindness, he may be able to take up his former duties. Thou, Who with Father and the Holy Spirit, liveth and reigneth God world without end. Amen.

If the illness is to last for some time, the sacrament gives to the sick person the necessary grace to endure his sickness in the spirit of holiness; it also remits to some extent the temporal punishment that is due to sin. There have not been wanting some theologians in the past who have held that, if received with great faith, it remits all temporal punishment due to sin, and in case of death, prepares the soul for heaven.

In this sacrament, sins are not remitted in virtue of an act of jurisdiction or by judicial sentence, as they are in the Sacrament of Penance. Why? Because with serious illness there is the possibility of passing into another community; that is, from the Church Militant to the Church Suffering or the Church Triumphant. The soul particularly in danger of death is about to go before the throne of the Eternal Judge and, therefore, to Him alone is reserved the jurisdiction or the judgment of the Sacrament of the Anointing of the Sick. That too is why, in the administration of this sacrament, there is more of the imprecatory form of prayer than in Penance. The

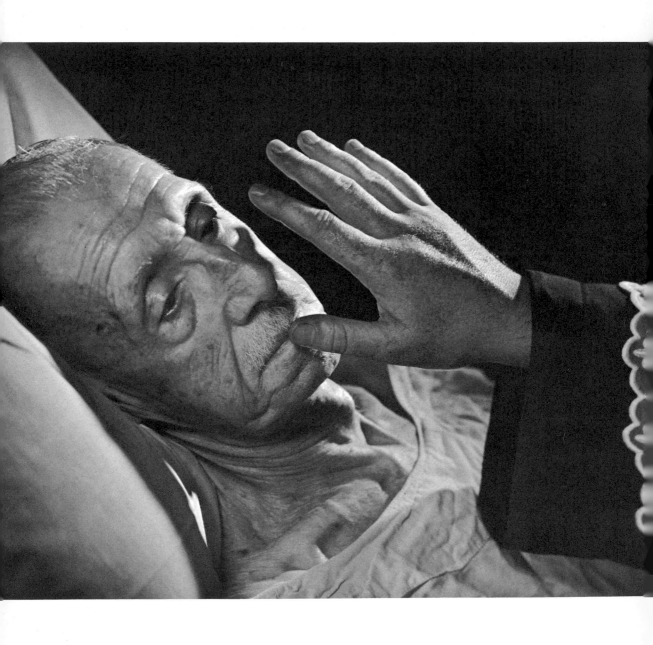

priest puts the prayer in the form of a petition because he is exercising his power only as a delegate of the Church Militant. In the Sacrament of Penance, the priest said: "I absolve you from your sins"; in the Sacrament of the Anointing of the Sick, "May the Lord forgive you any sins, etc." The measure of the distribution of grace here is left entirely to the merciful Love of God.

Because oil is used in the sacrament, it must not be forgotten that oil has a double purpose—strengthening and illumination or enlightenment. The aspect of strengthening has already been mentioned, but enlightenment also comes with this sacrament: it sheds a new outlook on the meaning of death. Many who receive this sacrament have the fear of death taken away from them, and may even desire it, as St. Paul said: "I desire to be dissolved and be with Christ."

This comes from a higher wisdom of the soul, because it has been purified of the remains of sin. Just as we see what is outside a window more clearly when the window has been washed, so too, our soul more clearly sees the purpose of life once the senses and soul have been purified. Saints very often undergo in life, through a great penance, what is called a "dark night of the soul." Thanks to this dark night, they then arrive at a kind of mystical union with God, or even a mystical espousal. Thanks to the anointing of this sacrament, one may also pass through a dark night of the soul, but in a much shorter period of time, and one looks forward to mystical union with Christ. Therefore, there can take place in the soul, in a very short space of time, both the purgative and illuminative way at the last moments of life: a cleansing of the soul and a greater vision of the glory and beauty of God.

The spiritual life would be terrible if the Good Lord had not instituted this sacrament for an illness, which is a rehearsal for the final battle of life. Thanks to it, the Church takes us in her maternal arms and shows us heaven saying:

> My children, here is your fatherland. Come with me. If it be God's Will, we will cross over this arid desert of life together, and we will confide you to the angels who will carry you through to your eternal repose.

The Viaticum

The Sacrament of the Anointing of the Sick is not the sacrament of the dying or, in the strict sense of the term, the "last sacrament." In the Liturgy

of the Church, the Sacrament of the Anointing is given before the Eucharist; when the latter is administered to the dying it becomes the "last sacrament." This is very fitting, for the Sacrament of the Eucharist has reference to the body as well as to the soul. Our Blessed Lord said that those who received Him in the Eucharist would be assured of the resurrection of the body. Furthermore, in the Mass there is a prayer immediately before Communion, which begs that the Eucharist "may be to me a safeguard for body and soul, and a remedy."

When given to those who are dying, the Eucharist is called Viaticum, which means "going with you" on the way to eternity. The Eucharist deposits in our body "a seed of immortality." It is a provision for the journey to eternity, when one is at the door of death. The Church makes its reception at this moment a matter of grave obligation, even more strict than the anointing of the sick.

The Viaticum received in danger of death, just as the Eucharist received in life, is social in its implications. There is not merely the union of Christ and the soul, but there is also the union of the sick with the whole Church. The dying person, if he is in a state of grace, is leaving the Church Militant on earth for either the Church Triumphant in heaven or the Church Suffering in purgatory. Hence, when a priest places the Eucharist on the tongue of the recipient, he says: "Receive, brother, [or sister] the Viaticum of Our Lord Jesus Christ that He may preserve thee from the malignant enemy and bring thee to everlasting life." The reference to "brother" or "sister" refers to the family and the fellowship of the Church and the saints. There should even be a solemnity about the last Communion, as there is about the First Communion. The family should gather about the one who receives the Viaticum, and its solemnity is increased when administered by the pastor himself who is the head of the parochial community.

The Catholic who is dying is never lonely because there is another rite connected with the Viaticum; namely, the commending of the soul to God. The priest gives him a crucifix to kiss while an invocation is said to the Cross: "We adore Thee, O Christ, and we bless Thee, because by Thy Holy Cross Thou has redeemed the world." As the moment of death approaches there is the official discharge to the dying:

> Go forth, Christian soul, out of this world, in the Name of God, the Father Almighty, Who created thee; in the Name of Jesus Christ, the Son of the Living God, Who suffered for thee; in the Name of the Holy Spirit, Who has poured forth upon thee. . . . May thy place be this day in peace and thy abode in holy Sion.

Then the Church calls on the angels and the saints:

> May the Angels lead thee into Paradise. At thy coming, may the Martyrs receive thee and lead thee into the holy city, Jerusalem. May the choir of Angels receive thee, and with Lazarus, who was once poor, mayst thou have eternal rest.

Death is one of the penalties for sin but, when accepted, it becomes an atonement also for sin. Every Christian knows that it is not just a happy life that one must seek for, but also a happy death. Hence, he prays that he may be fortified by the sacraments, and that he may be fully conscious when he receives the last rites, in order that he may, as it were, peer through the door of heaven to his eternal reward.

V I

THE SACRAMENT
OF HOLY ORDERS

Because man lives in a society of free men, there must be some government and order to make justice prevail. Since there is the order of
grace above creature, it too must have degrees, order, hierarchy, and
government; this Christ supplied in the Sacrament of Holy Orders with its
three ascending levels of deaconship, priesthood, and episcopacy.

Our Blessed Lord is the Mediator between God and Man, being both
God and man. But in order to mediate His redemption, He desires human
instruments between Himself and the world, each of whom will be "the
minister and dispenser of the Mysteries of God" (I CORINTH. 4:1). And so,
some men are appointed by God to deliver the sacraments to others, just
as in human societies one group serves and ministers to another:

> The purpose for which any high priest is chosen from among his
> fellow-men, and made a representative of men in their dealings
> with God, is to offer gifts and sacrifices in expiation of their sins.
>
> (HEB. 5:11)

The Call from God

In the fifth chapter of *Hebrews*, verse four, there is written: "His vocation comes from God, as Aaron's did; nobody can take on himself such a privilege as this." When a priest receives the call from God, something happens to his soul, like that which happened to Peter in his barque one dark night when Christ entered it. The young man with a vocation reacts as did Peter: "Depart from me, O Lord, for I am a sinful man." There is a double tension: one of attraction to the divine, the other, subtraction, because of one's own unworthiness; a desire to approach the All-Holy, and a shrinking because of one's own sense of inadequacy.

Then begins a minimum of six years of difficult study and moral and spiritual discipline, as one asks himself a thousand times if he is worthy. Either with the crucifix that hangs on the wall of his simple room, or to the crucifix on his desk, he carries on a constant dialogue.

The seminarian knows how human he is, and yet, like Christ on the Cross, suspended between heaven and earth, abandoned by one and rejected by the other, the world expects him to be more than human. Called to be as pure and as holy as an angel, he is conscious of his own weakness, bearing about as he does the rich treasure in a frail vessel. And yet he must fulfill the words of his Master: "Thou hast sent me into the world on thy errand, and I have sent them into the world on my errand" (JOHN 17:18). From now on, he no longer takes the short breaths of the world; he must draw in strength from the world of the spirit.

The Priest and Celibacy

Our Lord wished to have a group of men who would have the freedom to give full time to His service; hence He ordained in order that they who served the altar were to live by the altar. Celibacy in the Latin Rite stresses this quality of total dedication. The priest is a celibate in order that he might not have the cares of family and, therefore, not be afraid to minister to people in plague or to give the last rites to soldiers dying in battle. St. Paul, speaking of celibacy as a spur to undivided service, writes: "And I would have you free from concern. He who is unmarried is concerned with God's claim, asking how he is to please God" (I CORINTH. 7:32).

Chastity, however, is not something cold or negative. It is, as Francis Thompson called it, "a passionless passion, a wild tranquility." A man cannot live without love, though he can live without romantic love or the Eros. The divine command, "increase and multiply" (GEN. 1:28) may be verified

108

not only with reference to the body, but also to the soul. There can be increase of man in the cultural, moral, and religious spheres. The priest is called a "father," because he begets souls in Christ. As St. Paul wrote to the Galatians: "My little children, I am in travail over you afresh, until I can see Christ's image formed in you" (GAL. 4:19). The purer the mirror of his humanity is, the better he reflects the image of Christ.

Though a priest is called a father, nevertheless, he is also a "mother" of children. Our Blessed Lord used two analogies to describe His attitude toward the city that He loved, and also to all humanity. He said that He loved Jerusalem as a hen who gathers her chickens, but the city refused His love. The night of the Last Supper, He used the similitude of a mother about to bring forth a child, implying that He would be in labor in His Crucifixion, but would bring forth new life in His Resurrection.

The Ordination of the Priest

The dress of the priest takes one back to the classical days of Greece and Rome, when the Church became the spiritual Israel. The early clergy wore no distinctive dress, but rather clothed themselves in the garb of the ordinary people. Later on when the classical Roman dress began to be superseded by the dress of the barbarians, the conservativeness of religion asserted itself and, in consequence, the priest wore vestments which were no longer in secular use.

When the deacons enter the cathedral to be vested, they wear an amice, which was originally a white linen kerchief worn about the neck and the shoulders. When he put it on his head and shoulders, he said the prayer: "Place, O Lord, the helmet of salvation on my head to the defeat of diabolical invasion." Over the amice, he wears the alb, which was the original Roman tunic with long sleeves, around the waist of which he ties the cincture which is the symbol of chastity.

Over the alb is worn a maniple, which in the early days of the Greeks and Romans was a kind of handkerchief worn on the left forearm, used at meals for wiping mouth and hands. The consul during the Roman Empire used it as a sign to start the races in the circus. The Church first used it to wipe communion vessels and hands in the celebration of the Mass. The symbolism of the maniple is to remind the priest of the bonds which once held the hands of the Savior. This is signified in the prayer which is offered when the maniple is put on, begging that the cares and sorrows of earthly life should be borne with patience in view of heavenly reward.

Now we come to two vestments which are worn by deacons when they

109

come to the altar for ordination; namely, the stole and the chasuble. The stole originally was a loose robe worn by the ancients, and in this sense the word is still used by the English poets. Thus, Milton pictures Melancholy as having "a sable stole of cypress lawn, over her decent shoulders drawn."

In the Old Testament, the Levites were described as being clad in stoles when conducting the sacred Ark to Jerusalem. In the *Book of the Apocalypse,* the saints are "clothed in white stoles." The stole is worn only by deacons, priests, and bishops, but each wears it in a different way, and it is associated with sacred orders. When, however, the deacon enters the Church, the stole is carried only on one shoulder, while over the left arm the deacon carries a folded chasuble. In the right hand, he bears a lighted candle, and in the cincture is a linen cloth, which will eventually be used for tying the hands, after they have been anointed with oil.

During the ceremony of ordination, the bishop draws a part of the stole which rests at the back of the candidate's neck over the breast and lays the two ends crosswise. The chasuble which he carries and which is a symbol of charity, is folded at the beginning of the ordination ceremony, as an indication that the one who wears it is not a priest. At a later point in the ceremony, the chasuble is unfolded. The symbolism of this is that, in the first part of the Mass, the deacon is made a priest and given the power of offering sacrifice to God. In the second part of the ceremony, the chasuble is then let down when he is empowered to preach and forgive sins. This indicates the more complete powers of the priest.

St. John Chrysostom explains well the reason why priests wear different vestments at the altar than on the street: "When you see a priest offering the Sacrifice, do not think of it as if it were *he* that is doing this; it is the Hand of Christ invisibly stretched forth." The priest is really only a tool, but he is a tool in the sense that Aristotle called man a living tool. The vestments hide and submerge his own personality so that men may know it is Christ Who teaches, Who governs, and Who sanctifies.

The Call from the Bishop

No man can be ordained unless he has been called by Christ through the bishop. When Our Lord called His Apostles, He called them by name, and this ceremony is repeated in the Sacrament of Holy Orders. The Latin rite begins by the archdeacon presenting the deacons, saying that the Holy Church asks them to be elevated to the rank of priest. The bishop,

110

reading from the Pontifical, reminds them of the old custom of the Church, when the people were consulted concerning the life, conduct, and morals of the clergy before they were elevated to the priesthood. He then tells them that as Moses elected seventy elders from the different tribes of Israel to aid him in the government of the people of the Old Law, as Our Lord chose seventy-two disciples to preach the Gospel, so are they to aid the bishop in the sacred ministry of sacrificing, blessing, presiding, preaching, and baptizing.

The bishop seated on the faldstool at the middle of the altar begins the ceremony of ordination. The archdeacon summons the future priests with these words: "Let all those who are to be ordained priests come forward." As they advance, their names are read out one by one. Each answers: *Adsum* ("I am present") and then steps forward. The calling by name means that there shall be no intruders and that the priesthood is a divine vocation or calling. Our Lord "calls His sheep by name" even now as He did in Galilee.

After the bishop calls out the names, there follows a very solemn warning, that they come not under false pretenses, that they are under no penalties of the Church, and that they be not illegitimate:

> Most Reverend Father and Lord in Christ, [name of Bishop] by the grace of God and the Apostolic See, Bishop of [diocese] commands and charges under pain of excommunication that no one here present for the purpose of taking Orders, shall presume to come forward for ordination under any pretext, if he be irregular, excommunicate in any law or by judicial sentence, under interdict or suspension, illegitimate or infamous, or in any other way disqualified, or of any other diocese, unless he has the license of the bishop; and that none of the ordained shall depart until the Mass is over and the Bishop's blessing has been received.

The archdeacon then bids the bishop to ordain these deacons "to the burden of the priesthood." The phrase that is used is *onus* or burden. The priesthood and the episcopacy are both called burdens, not honors. This is because the terrific burden or responsibility of saving souls entrusted to them is laid upon them there. Such was the idea given to Moses when he complained to the Lord: "Must I carry a whole people like a weight on my back?" (Num. 11:11).

As if still hesitant as to whether or not the deacons should be ordained, the bishop then asks the archdeacon the question: "Do you know them to

111

be worthy?" To which he answers: "So far as human frailty allows one to know, I do know, and I testify that they are worthy to undertake the burden of this office." The bishop then answers, *"Deo Gratias"* ("Thanks be to God").

Moral certitude about the worthiness of the candidates is required like the certitude that Moses was to have when God told him to gather seventy men among the ancients of Israel whom he *knew* to be worthy. This concern for the worthiness of the candidates has always been present in the Old Testament and the New, for St. Paul tells Timothy that before he ordains any priests he should be very certain of their worthiness: "He must bear a good character, too, in the world's eyes; or he may fall into disrepute, and become a prey to the False Accuser" (I TIM. 3:7).

The bishop, as if not satisfied with assurance of the archdeacon, asks the people if they know any reason why the deacons should not be ordained. There follows a moment of silence, in which the people are given an opportunity to protest, if need be, against any one of the candidates.

The Prostration

The deacons now prostrate themselves flat upon the ground and become as dead men, while over them the Church, chanting the Litany of the Saints, invokes heaven to intercede, or pray for them, to be merciful to them, and to make them good priests.

The prostration of the deacons during the Litanies is a slightly different form of prayer than that which was used in the Old Testament, when the Jews generally stood to pray. It was only in times of great stress that they ever knelt (ACTS 7:59 and ACTS 9:40), such as when Stephen and Peter knelt. The Jews, however, did lay prostrate before the High Priest for a solemn blessing on the Day of Atonement (ECCLUS. 50:19–26), and as Our Lord did in the Agony in the Garden. But the reason for the kneeling is somewhat related to a prayer that went before, where the *ordinandi* were told "as they celebrate the mysteries of the Lord's death, they must be earnest in mortifying their members of all vices and concupiscence." Being prostrate is a symbol of their spiritual death, in which they die to their flesh and its concupiscences at the same time, that they invoke all the saints in heaven to let them have a resurrection worthy of being ministers of the Word.

As the body of Adam came from the slime of the earth, when God breathed into it a living soul, so each priest yielding his body to be an

112

instrument of Christ, prays fervently that it may never be a blunt instrument. Then when he rises from the ground, his hands are bound with a purificator, tied together in slavery, but that sweet slavery of love. With Paul he says: "I am alive; or rather, not I; it is Christ that lives in me" (GAL. 2:20).

The Laying on of Hands

The bishop lays hands on the priests without saying anything. When a bishop is consecrated, the hands of the consecrating prelates are laid on him with the words: "Receive the Holy Spirit," but in ordination, these words are omitted. This laying on or imposition of hands is what is called the "matter" of the sacrament, and is part of the ritual of other sacraments, like Baptism, Confirmation, Penance, and the Anointing of the Sick.

There are many instances in the Old Testament of laying on of hands. Jacob put his right hand on the head of Ephraim, and his left hand on the head of Manasse and pronounced a blessing (GEN. 48:14, 15). Aaron and his sons placed their hands on the heads of victims to be offered in sacrifice:

> He is to lay his hand on the head of the victim, and it is to be immolated at the entrance of the tabernacle that bears record of me, the priests who represent Aaron's family pouring its blood upon the altar.
>
> (LEV. 3:2)

God told Moses to lay his hand on Josue (NUM. 27:18) and Aaron after offering sacrifice. In the Old Testament, it signified that a victim or a person was dedicated to a holy purpose, and also that there was a flowing out of power from the one who laid on the hands.

Investiture of Priesthood

The bishop chants a preface invoking the Holy Spirit upon those who are to be ordained; then follows what is known as the "form" of the sacrament:

> We beseech Thee, Almighty Father, invest these Thy servants with the dignity of the priesthood. Do Thou renew in their hearts the spirit of holiness. Help them to be steadfast in the office of

114

second priestly rank received from Thee, O Lord, and to inspire others to strive for perfection by their example. May they become zealous fellow workers in our ministry. May they shine in all the Christian virtues, so that they will be able to give a good account of the stewardship entrusted to them, and finally attain the reward of everlasting life. Through the same Jesus Christ, Thy Son, Our Lord, Who lives and reigns with Thee, in the unity of the Holy Spirit, God forever and ever. Amen.

The bishop arranges the stole in the form of a cross over the chest, saying: "Take the yoke of the Lord, for His yoke is sweet and His burden light." Then he invests each with the chasuble, still unfolded, saying: "Receive, the vesture of priesthood, which is the symbol of charity. God is well able to increase charity in you and make perfect your works."

After the *Veni Creator Spiritus* has been sung, in which the Holy Spirit is invoked, the bishop proceeds to anoint the hands of each in the form of a cross. The bishop's right thumb is dipped in the oil of catechumens; with the oil he traces a cross with his right thumb, a line from the thumb of the right hand to the index finger of the left, and the other from the thumb of the left to the index finger of the right. Then he anoints the hands all over, and as he does so, he says: "Be pleased, O Lord, to consecrate and hallow these hands by this anointing and our blessing. Amen." He makes a sign over each saying: "Whatsoever they bless may be blessed, and whatsoever they consecrate may be consecrated and hallowed in the Name of Our Lord Jesus Christ."

In the Old Testament, the candidate was anointed with holy oil which, in the case of the high priest, was poured upon his head, but in the case of the other priests, it was merely put upon his forehead. The anointed hands of the priests are folded and tied together with a linen cloth, so as to allow the oil to penetrate into his hands. He then becomes Christ's bondsman (EPH. 3:1).

The Delivery of Instruments

The bishop now presents each of the newly ordained with a *chalice* containing wine and water, and a *paten* upon the chalice with a host. Because the anointed hands of the priest are bound, he touches with the fore and middle fingers both the paten and the cup of the chalice. During the ceremony the bishop says: "Receive the power to offer sacrifice to God and to celebrate Mass, both for the living and the dead in the name of Our Lord. Amen."

116

Concelebration

After the Offertory, the newly-ordained priests begin to celebrate Mass with the Bishop saying the prayers aloud with them. They even say the words of consecration with him. The meaning of the ceremony is that as the Apostles learned to celebrate Mass from Our Blessed Lord at the Last Supper; so too, in concelebrating with the bishop, the new priests learn a ritual from a successor of the Apostles. As the newly-ordained priests concelebrate with the bishop, so too, they receive communion, drinking from the same chalice, and consuming a host that was consecrated at the Mass.

The Commission to Absolve

Before the Communion prayer is read, the Mass is interrupted a second time to give the priests a new function in the Mystical Body of Christ. After the profession of faith, the bishop sits down and lays both hands on the head of each one kneeling before him, and says: "Receive the Holy Ghost; whose sins you shall forgive, they are forgiven them; and whose sins you shall retain, they are retained."

The bishop does not wear gloves for this second imposition, but he does for the first. The Mass is interrupted here, for the second time, to give the power *to forgive* sins, because this power was given by Our Lord at a time distinct from that of the authority *to offer the Mass.* The night of the Last Supper Our Lord ordained His priests, *after having offered* the sacrifice of *bread* and wine, saying: "Do this in commemoration of Me." But it was after His Resurrection that He gave them priestly power to forgive sins and the power of binding and loosing. This corresponds also to the double ceremony of the chasuble: first, the putting it on as folded for the pre-Resurrection power; and secondly, the unfolding, to indicate the giving of additional priestly powers of forgiveness. When the chasuble is unfolded, the bishop prays: "May the Lord clothe you with the robe of innocence."

The Promise of Obedience

The newly-ordained priests now come up for what is called the *stipulatio.* There is not a clasping of hands here, for that would signify equality. The hands, being the instruments of action and service, are put *inside* the bishop's hands to signify his will to be put at the service of the bishop. It is a commitment of the young priest to his father in Christ.

118

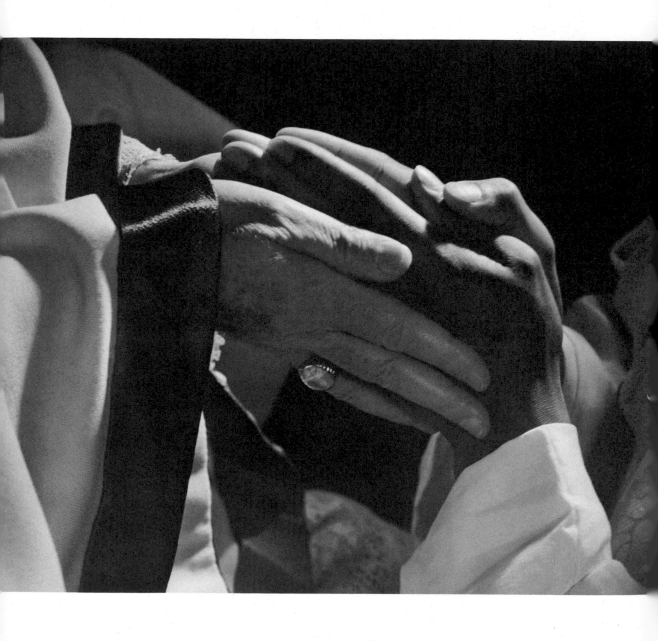

The Consecration of a Bishop

The bishop too must be called by the Vicar of Christ and cannot be consecrated without his express permission. The consecration ceremony begins with the question, "Have you the mandate?"; i.e., has the Holy Father, the successor of St. Peter, given us the authority to number this priest among the Apostles? Two things hang together there: apostolic succession and the Primacy of Peter. The night of the Last Supper when Our Lord consecrated His Apostles, He reminded them of how they were bound together in Peter, whom He had chosen as the rock, the leader and the first, not only in honor, but in jurisdiction.

What is very singular about the words of Our Lord is that He did not pray for all of the Apostles as equals: *He prayed for them in and through Peter.* It was through their oneness with Peter that they would share in His prayer of victory over the evil of the world. This is brought out in the way Our Lord addressed Peter in the second person singular in distinction to the Apostles whom He addressed in the second person plural:

> And the Lord said, Simon, Simon, behold, Satan has claimed power over you all, so that he can sift you like wheat: but I have prayed for thee, that thy faith may not fail, when, after a while, thou hast come back to me, it is for thee to be the support of thy brethren.
>
> (LUKE 22:31, 32)

He told Peter that he would deny Him, but afterwards would return and be the support of his brethren.

When the Communists in China attempted to destroy the Church, they cleverly sought to insert a division between apostolic succession and the Primacy of Peter. Brainwashing a few bishops, they succeeded in inducing them to consecrate a few priests. The priests would then, because they were consecrated by bishops, be in the line of apostolic succession; the Communists thus hoped that the faithful would accept them. But because they had not the authority or the mandate from the Holy Father to do so, the Communists thereby denied the Primacy of Peter. As it turned out, the Catholics refused to accept the bishops who may have been in the line of apostolic succession, but certainly were not embraced in the prayer of Christ for Peter.

Both apostolic succession and the recognition of the Primacy of Peter go together. It is very much like the problem of lighting a city by electricity. Suppose in this city there were a thousand houses. The wire from one house ran only a foot, another twenty feet, another five hundred feet, another fifteen hundred feet, another eighteen hundred. But suppose that the dynamo that supplied all of this power was about two thousand feet away from the houses. It would follow that none of the copper cables would be able to light a house; regardless of how close they came to the dynamo, they would not be in actual contact with power.

So it is with the transmission of priestly authority and power. Any organization which starts today, or which started fifty years ago, or five hundred years ago, or one thousand years ago, is incapable of transmitting the divine power of Christ's Passion, unless there is a contact with Christ Himself and under the conditions Christ laid down. As in biology, life comes from life, so in theology, divine life comes from divine life. An unbroken succession of authority and power is essential for the divinization of souls in the twentieth century. The bishops, who are successors of the Apostles, are one in Peter and his successors, to whom alone Christ promised that the "faith would fail not."

During the ceremony, after the bishop-elect has been interrogated concerning his fidelity, submission, and obedience to God and the Church and all the truths of faith, the consecrating prelate accompanied by two co-consecrators tells him at the beginning of Mass: "It is the duty of a bishop to judge, interpret, consecrate, ordain, offer, baptize, and confirm." After all the saints of heaven have been invoked in the Litany, the consecrator and his co-consecrators successively touch with both hands the head of the bishop elect saying: "Receive the Holy Spirit." These words constitute the matter of the sacrament. Then comes the prayer that is known as the form:

> Be propitious, O Lord, to our supplications, and bestowing the abundance of sacerdotal grace upon this Thy servant, pour upon him the power of Thy blessing, through Our Lord Jesus Christ Who liveth and reigneth with Thee in the unity of the Holy Ghost.

He anoints the head of the consecrated kneeling before him, making first the sign of the cross on the crown, and then anointing the whole crown of the head, saying: "May the head be anointed and consecrated by heavenly benediction in the pontifical order in the Name of the Father ✠, in the Name of the Son ✠, and of the Holy Ghost. ✠ Amen."

After a prayer, the newly-consecrated bishop has his hands anointed

with chrism in the form of a cross. The consecrator draws two lines with the thumb of his right hand, one from the thumb of the right hand to the index finger of the left, the other from the thumb of the left hand to the index finger of the right; then the whole palm of the consecrated is anointed while these words are said by the consecrator:

> May these hands be anointed with the sanctified oil and the chrism of sanctification; as Samuel anointed David to be king and prophet, so may they be anointed and consecrated in the Name of the Father ✠, the Son ✠, and the Holy Spirit ✠. We make the Sign of the Holy Cross of Our Savior, Jesus Christ, Who redeemed us from death and led us to the Kingdom of Heaven.

The newly-consecrated Bishop concelebrates the Mass with his consecrator, even drinking of the same chalice. Passing over many other details for want of space, his newly-acquired powers are symbolized in his crozier, mitre, ring, and gloves.

Because the bishop is the father of a spiritual family, or a shepherd, he is given a shepherd's staff. Our Blessed Lord called His bishops and priests to be both shepherds and fishermen. Because the bishop is the spouse of the Church, he is given a ring to indicate that espousal. Because he is to be a mediator of the Old and the New Testament, he wears the helmet of salvation, which is the mitre. Because he hopes to receive the blessing of the Heavenly Father, as Jacob received the blessing—thanks to covered hands—he wears gloves.

After the enthronement, the consecrated bishop then gives His blessing. He goes to the Epistle corner of the altar, kneels and sings, "For many years"; then going to the middle of the altar, he again kneels and sings in a higher voice, "For many years." As he approaches the one who consecrated him, kneeling a third time he sings in a still higher voice, "For many years." Then he receives the kiss of peace from the bishop who consecrated him and from the other bishops.

The keynote of the bishop's mission is not administration, but life—the communication of the life that Christ brought to this earth. If there is administration—and administration there must be—it is in the service of divine life. All the bishop's powers are directed to the formation of Christ in the souls of the people. Others may be instructors, but in each diocese there is only one father, the bishop. As St. Paul said: "Yes, you may have ten thousand schoolmasters in Christ, but not more than one father; it was I that begot you in Jesus Christ, when I preached the gospel to you" (I CORINTH. 4:15).

124

Father he is, because he has the right and power to administer all the sacraments. Father he is, because his government is in the exercise of the Heavenly Fatherhood. Father he is, because his domain is universal. He is sent first to the world and then, only for jurisdictional reasons, assigned to a diocese. The reason is that the universal Church is not the sum total of all the dioceses throughout the world; rather, the dioceses derive from the Church, not the other way around. The Church preceded them. It has been founded entirely on the episcopacy and its mission to make disciples of all nations. The bishop is not primarily the pastor of a single flock. He is a pastor of the universal Church in union with the supreme head of the Church, Peter and his successors. Hence, one of the primary responsibilities of the bishop is to the missions of the Church.

The bishop is a father also because he alone has the power to generate priests, though priests have the power to generate Christians. No priest has the power to ordain another priest, though he has the power to beget the faithful.

The priest, or the bishop, in his daily round, is a minister of God, a messenger from another world, bringing upward to God prayers and adoration, and bringing down from God graces and blessings to the people. He is to lay hold of anything and anybody who wills to be ennobled by the grace of God, whether it be a dishonest Zacheus, in a tree out of curiosity, or an accountant, like Matthew at his desk, or a fellow-traveler with the enemy. His feet are scarred from thorns, where the lost sheep or the fallen-aways have become entangled; they are to be dusty from searching and sweeping for the lost coin of spiritual wanderers.

From proud tempers, he will meet ridicule and insult; from the blasphemer, blows; from the oppressed, entreaty; from the poor, a pleading. But he is one who after every contact should inspire others to say as the woman at the well: "Come and have sight of a man who has told me the whole story of my life; can this be the Christ?" (JOHN 4:29)

No case to him is hopeless. Every soul must be to him like the drop of water in the ugly gutter which, looked at closely, reflects the deep serious blue of the far off sky. He knows that he cannot convince others that he comes from another world, unless he acts as if he had been there. The world may see his acts, but they do not know his thoughts.

When he mounts the altar, he carries with him all the woes and the wounds of the world. His feet, that walk up the altar steps, must have on them the imprint of the homeless, the refugees, and the wanderers of the earth. His face, as he kisses the altar, should bear within it the faces of those whose eyes are blasted before furnaces, darkened in salt mines, wet with the tears of grief and furrowed with the worry of sin. His vestments should be heavy with the millions of souls who know not Christ and yet who are clinging to his vestments, hoping for they know not what. As his fingers lift up the body and blood of Christ, he asks that all the sufferings of the world be united with Christ and that no pain go to waste.

He will feel sad, because he knows how men are bitterly losing the good in their lives, but he will be consoled knowing that God is near them even if they know it not; around them, even though they perceive it not. In his conversations, he will seek to lift flippancy into reverence, controversy into thoughtfulness, frivolity into practical life. When he mounts the pulpit, he should be a speaking crucifix.

But above all, he will not be just a priest, but a victim, for Christ was that, offering Himself for our salvation. There will be no tear shed by fellow man that does not bedew his own cheek; no mourning parent who will not pierce his heart with grief; no sheep who will be without a shepherd. And because he knows that he is too often a priest offering Christ, and too seldom a victim sharing His Cross, he will daily pray to the Mother of Christ:

> "Since you formed Christ the priest and victim in thy body, form
> Him, I beg thee in my heart. Do this, that in addition to the
> words of consecration at Mass, I may say them, as thou didst
> gaze on thy Son on the Cross: 'This is *my* body; this is *my* blood.'
> Then I shall, through thy help, live and die with Him."

VII

THE SACRAMENT OF MATRIMONY

Love exists on three different levels: the sex level, the friendship-love, and the sacramental.

Sex love alone is directed toward another for the sake of pleasure which the other person gives the ego. The partner is regarded as one of the opposite sex, instead of as a person. The infatuation associated with it is nothing but the boundless desire of self-centeredness to express itself at all costs. Because it cares only for its own rapture and its own fulfillment, such love quickly turns to hate when no longer satisfied.

Over and above sex love, there is *personal* love. Personal love includes sex in marriage, but in its essence, it is based on the objective value of another person. The other person may be loved for artistic or moral excellence, or because of a common, sympathetic interest. Personal love exists wherever there is reciprocity, duality, and understanding. This kind of love can exist with carnal love in marriage, or quite apart from carnal love, for there is no direct connection between the flesh and love. It is possible to be in love without there being physical attraction, as it is possible to have physical attraction without being in love. Personal love is in the will, not in the body.

In personal love, there is no substitution of persons possible; *this* person is loved, and not another. But in carnal or erotic love, since there is not of necessity a love for another person, but only a love of self, it is possible to find a substitute for the one who gives pleasure. Sex love substitutes one occasion of pleasure for the other, but real love knows no substitution. No one can take the place of a mother.

Beyond each of these two is *Christian love,* which loves everyone either as a potential or actual child of God, redeemed by Christ; it is a love which loves without even a hope of return. It loves the other, not because of attractiveness, or talents, or sympathy, but because of God. To the Christian, a person is one for whom I must sacrifice myself, not one who must exist for my sake. Sex love demands carnal reciprocity; personal love finds it difficult to survive without it; but Christian love requires no reciprocity. Its inspiration is Christ, Who loved us while we were sinners and, therefore, unlovable.

The sanctity of married life is not something which takes place *alongside* marriage, but *by* and *through* marriage. The vocation to marriage is a vocation to happiness which comes through holiness and sanctity. Unity of two in one flesh is not something that God tolerates, but something that He wills. Because He wills it, He sanctifies the couple through its use. Instead of diminishing in any way the union of their spirits with one another, it contributes to their ascension in love. The sacrament which sanctifies this kind of love is Matrimony.

Marriage: A Symbol of the Nuptials of Christ and the Church

Marriage as a sacrament belongs to an entirely different order than the mere union of man and woman through a civil contract. It basically regards a husband and wife as symbols of another marriage; namely, the nuptials of Christ and His Church.

The analogy of the heavenly nuptials goes back to the Old Testament, where God appears as the bridegroom, and Israel appears as the bride. When God becomes incarnate in Christ, He called Himself, and was called, the Bridegroom; it is the new Israel, or the Church, which becomes His bride or His spouse. It is often forgotten that our Blessed Lord called Himself a Bridegroom. When Our Lord was asked why the disciples of John fasted, but His own did not, He answered: "Can you expect the men of the bridegroom's company to go fasting, while the bridegroom is still with them? As long as they have the bridegroom with

them, they cannot be expected to fast" (MARK 2:19). John the Baptist called himself "the friend of the bridegroom," or what might be, in modern language, the "best man." The title of Bridegroom, which belonged to Christ, was shared by no other, as John himself said: "The bride is for the bridegroom; but the bridegroom's friend, who stands by and listens to him, rejoices too, rejoices at hearing the bridegroom's voice" (JOHN 3:29). ·

On the other hand, the wife's relationship to the husband is the relationship of the Church to Christ. That is why when St. Paul speaks of marriage he says, "Those words are a high mystery . . . applying . . . to Christ and His Church" (EPH. 5:32). The ultimate consummation of this espousal of Christ and His Church will be after the resurrection, when the Church "without spot or wrinkle" will appear as a bride adorned for her husband or as the "spouse of the Lamb" (APOC. 21:2, 9:1, 22:17).

The Sacrament of Matrimony is not a pious extra added to the marriage contract; it is rather the elevation of a natural marriage contract to the order of grace, in which the husband loves the wife, as Christ loves the Church, and the wife loves the husband as the Church loves Christ. The husband and wife are not just a symbol of the union of Christ and the Church; they enjoy a real participation in that union. As Christ lives in the Church and the Church in Christ, so the husband lives in the wife and the wife in the husband, and the two are in one flesh.

The role of the priest in the sacrament is to ratify, to witness, and to bestow the Church's official blessing on those whom she now empowers to furnish new members to Christ's Mystical Body. This is the one sacrament in which the contracting parties are the ministers of the sacrament to each other. In the words of one to the other and in the giving of the hand to each other, there is the mutual surrender of rights and the acceptance of duties. But to be a sacrament, a representative of the Church must be there to witness it.

Matrimony, in virtue of the mutual inherence of man and woman, is a little cameo reflecting the greater espousal of Christ and His Body, the Church. The word "body" is used throughout Scripture to signify not only the human body, but also the Eucharistic Body or the Real Presence of Christ, and also the Mystical Body which is the Church. All three are in some way united. In the marriage ceremony the bridegroom, though he does not say so expressly, is by implication saying to the bride: "This is my body; this is my blood." The bride says the same to him. It is a kind of "consecration" on a lower level. When during the Mass they hear the words of Consecration, "This is My Body; This is My Blood," they give themselves to Christ in the same action, they give themselves to one another. The epistle of their marriage Mass reminds them of this bond to the Church:

> Wives must obey their husbands as they would obey the Lord. The man is the head to which the woman's body is united, just as Christ is the head of the Church, He, the Savior, on whom the safety of His body depends; and women must owe obedience at all points to their husbands, as the Church does to Christ.
>
> (EPH. 5:22-24)

The man is the "head" of the wife, as Christ is the Head of the Church. What did Christ do for the Church as her Head? He died for it. Hence, husbands must show love to their wives. The "headship" is not overlordship, but love unto sacrifice. The wife, in her turn, will show to the husband the devotion and love the Church does to Christ.

As further evidence of how seriously the Church takes marriage as the symbol of Christ and the Church, St. Thomas Aquinas makes a distinction between a marriage that is merely *ratified* at the altar, and a marriage that is *ratified and consummated,* when husband and wife become two in one flesh. The Church has always made this distinction in her Canon Law concerning marriage. A marriage that is merely ratified at the altar, but not consummated, represents the union of *Christ with the soul through grace.* A marriage ratified at the altar and consummated in the marriage act symbolizes the union of *Christ and the Church.*

The marriage that is ratified only, is a symbol of a personal union of the soul with Christ through grace. This union can be broken by sin. If, therefore, a husband and wife separated immediately after the marriage at the church door, and never consummated their marriage, that marriage would be breakable under certain conditions, because it is only the symbol of the union of the soul and grace. But the marriage bond of a baptized husband and wife which has been consummated is absolutely unbreakable, as the union of Christ and the Church is unbreakable.

The Administration of the Sacrament

The sacrament when administered at a nuptial Mass takes place before the Mass commences, and begins with an exhortation to the couple. A sample exhortation often appears in liturgical books, though it is not part of the sacrament; a priest may and should prepare his own sermonette to the lovers.

After the young couple have been reminded of the nature of the sacrament and its obligations, the priest asks the groom: "[Name] will you take [Name] here present for your lawful wife, according to the rite of our Holy Mother Church?" The bridegroom answers: "I will." Then the bride is asked: "[Name] will you take [Name] here present for your lawful husband, according to the rite of our Holy Mother the Church?" The bride answers: "I will." The priest bids them join their right hands; then first the groom and then the bride says: "I take you [name] for my lawful wife [husband] to have and to hold, from this day forward, for better, for worse, for richer, for poorer, in sickness and in health, until death do us part."

Then follows the confirmation of the marriage bond in which the priest says: "Your marriage contract, I, by the authority of the Church, now seal and bless in the Name of the Father, and of the Son, and of the Holy Ghost." When the ring is blessed the priest says: "Bless, O Lord, this ring, which we are blessing in Thy Name so that she who wears it keeping

132

faith with her husband in unbroken loyalty may ever remain at peace with Thee, obedient to Thy Will, and may live with him always in mutual love through Christ Our Lord. Amen."

Because the sacrament represents the heavenly espousals, the Church practically asks the bride and groom what guarantee they will give that they love one another until death. If they say, "We pledge our word," the Church will answer: "Words and pacts can be broken, as the history of the world too well proves." If they say, "We give the pledge of a ring," the Church will answer: "Rings can be broken and lost, and with them the memory of the promise." It is only when the ring which is given becomes a symbol of the love of Christ and His Church, does the Church

unite in marriage. Eternal salvation is involved in their reception of the Sacrament. Their lives become bonded at the altar, sealed with the seal of the cross, signed with the sign of the Eucharist which they both receive into their souls, as a pledge of their unity in the spirit, which is the foundation of their unity in the flesh.

The Bride in the Marriage Ceremony

In a nuptial Mass, the bride and bridegroom come to the altar immediately after the *Pater Noster*. The prayer that is said here is for the bride. There is no special prayer said for the bridegroom. Part of the prayer is as follows:

> Look in Thy mercy upon this Thy handmaid, who is to be joined in wedlock and entreats protection and strength from Thee. May the yoke of love and of peace be upon her. True and chaste may she wed in Christ; and may she ever follow the pattern of holy women; and may she be dear to her husband like Rachel; wise like Rebecca; long-lived and faithful like Sara. May the author of deceit work none of his evil deeds within her. May she ever be knit to the Faith and to the commandments. May she be true to one husband, and fly from forbidden approaches. May she fortify her weakness by strong discipline. May she be grave in demeanor and honored for her modesty. May she be well taught in heavenly lore. May she be fruitful in offspring. May her life be good and sinless. May she win the rest of the blessed and the Kingdom of Heaven.

The bridegroom is now included in the prayer for the bride: "May they both see their children's children unto the third and fourth generation, and may they reach the old age which they desire. Through the same Christ, Our Lord."

The liturgy is very interesting in that it gives the emphasis to the bride. Even from a worldly point of view, the bride is the one who receives the attention in marriage. There are showers of gifts for the bride, but not always for the bridegroom. The marriage song is "Here Comes the Bride," but there is no song: "Here Comes the Bridegroom." Everyone, too, is interested in what the bride wears, not in what the bridegroom wears.

In Scripture, where there is the final marriage of the Church and Christ in heavenly glory after the end of the world, all the emphasis is upon the Bridegroom, Christ, and little upon the bride. It would seem as if time, human history, or the waiting for the Second Coming of Christ is the

134

season of the bride; but eternal glory is for the Bridegroom. In the *Book of Ruth,* where the final glory is typified and symbolized, there is emphasis only upon Boaz. The bride is quietly at home awaiting the coming of the groom. She does not appear in the ceremony at the gate. Though in worldly weddings and even in the liturgy of the Church, the bride steals the show, it is not so at the wedding of the Lamb in Heaven. There He becomes the center of attention. All the bride possesses is in Him, and through Him and with Him. In the *Book of the Apocalypse,* a long description of how the Bridegroom would be dressed is given, but there is only a very simple description of the bride: "Hers it is to wear linen of shining white; the merits of the saints are her linen" (Apoc. 19:8). The *Apocalypse* calls the final union of Christ and the Church the wedding of the Lamb, not the wedding of the bride.

An Unbreakable Bond

Because Matrimony images forth in the order of flesh the union of Christ and the Church, it follows that it is unbreakable. In the Incarnation, Our Blessed Lord took human nature which was the beginning of His Mystical Body, not for three years, nor for thirty-three, but for all eternity. So man and woman, reflecting the eternal union of Christ and the Church, take one another until death do they part. The enduring character of marriage, "until death do us part," is evident even in the natural order, where there are but two words in the vocabulary of love, "you" and "always." "You" because love is unique; "always" because love is enduring. No one ever said: "I will love you for two years and six months." That is why all love songs have the ring of eternity about them. No power on earth can fragment that which is one, and husband and wife are made one in marriage. To try and make of them two single and separate individuals, as they were before marriage, is actually to make them fragments of a joint personality, like unto Solomon taking his sword and threatening to divide the babe.

Other evidence of the unbreakable character of marriage is to be found in the way Scripture speaks of marriage—never interpreting it in terms of sex, but always in terms of "knowledge": "And now Adam had knowledge of his wife, Eve, and she conceived" (Gen. 4:1). When the angel Gabriel announced to the Blessed Mother that she was to be the Mother of God, she asked: "How can that be, since I have no knowledge of man?" (Luke 1:35). St. Paul later on enjoins husbands to "possess your wives in knowledge."

135

Why is marriage in the Bible related to knowledge? It is in order to reveal the close union of man and wife. There is nothing in the universe that reveals a deeper union than that of the mind and that which it knows. When the mind knows a *flower* or a *tree,* it possesses these objects within itself. They are not identified with intellect: they are distinct from it, and nothing can separate them.

Because marriage is knowledge, it follows that it demands fidelity. Suppose a student, until he entered college, never knew the soliloquy of Hamlet. Once he came to *know* it, he would always be dependent on the college which had given him that knowledge. That is why he calls his college his "beloved mother" or his *alma mater;* she caused something to happen in him which was unique. He could go on enjoying the soliloquy all the days of his life, but he could never reacquire it.

So too, when a husband and wife come to know one another in marriage they may enjoy the union many times, but they can never again reacquire that knowledge. As long as time endures, it is this man who has made her a woman; it is this woman who has made him a man. A deep bond of relationship is established between the two, though not in the same order as the bond between the mother and the child.

This suggests a union between man and woman that is much more personal than carnal. Both man and woman, in the moment of knowing, receive a gift which neither ever knew before, and which can never be known again, except by repetition. The resulting psychic changes are as great as the somatic. A woman can never again return to virginity; the man can never again return to ignorance. Something has happened to make them one, and from that oneness comes fidelity so long as either has a body. Sex is never just an "experience"; it is a bond registered through eternity.

The great advantage of the marriage vow which relates husband and wife to the union of Christ and the Church, is that it guards the couple against allowing the moods of a moment to override reason. There is no other way to control capricious solicitation except by a vow. Once its inviolable character is recognized, an impulse is subject to probing one's own faults and the making of new efforts to deepen love and understanding.

The Begetting of Children

The union of husband and wife also imitates the Church in its fecundity. In the union of Christ and the Church, there is spiritual fecundity (increase in conversions); in the human marriage, there is corporal fe-

136

cundity. As the Church begets children out of the womb of the baptismal font, fecundated by the Holy Spirit, so husband and wife beget children. Hence, in the prayer of the Church during the sacrament, God is asked: "May they both see their children's children unto the third and fourth generation, and may they reach the old age which they desire. Through the same Christ, Our Lord."

If the ultimate aim of the union of man and woman is not life, then there can be only one alternative, namely, death. The child is the physical expression of the fecundity of the Godhead, in which the Father is the source of the eternal generation of the Son. The gift of generation is not a push from below; it is a gift from above. It comes not from the animals of the field, but rather it descends from heaven as a reflection of the Father saying to His Son: "This day have I begotten Thee."

This primary end of Matrimony brings the couple in relationship to the Divine Trinity, as the duality of husband and wife ends in the begetting of children, the third term in their love. This is in keeping with the very nature of love, which may be defined as a *mutual self-giving which ends in self-recovery*. All love must be a *giving*, for without a giving there is not goodness; without self-outpouring there is no love. In marriage, love is first a mutual self-giving for love's greatest joy is to gird its loins and serve.

But if love were only mutual self-giving, it would end in self-exhaustion, or else become a flame in which both would be consumed. Mutual self-giving also implies self-recovery. The mutual self-giving of husband and wife, like the love of earth and tree, becomes fruitful in new love. There is a mutual self-surrender as they overcome their individual impotence by filling up, at the store of the other, the lacking measure. There is self-recovery as they beget not the mere sum of themselves, but a new life which makes them an earthly trinity. Love that is ever seeking to give, and is ever defeated by receiving, is the shadow of the Trinity on earth; therefore, a foretaste of heaven.

Behind the urge to procreate is the hidden desire of every human to participate in the eternal. Since man cannot do this in himself, he compensates for it by continuing life in another. Our inability to externalize ourselves is overcome by giving, with God's help, something immortal to the human race. Thus, the parents become co-creators with God, as the angel told Tobias:

> Then, when the third night is past, take the maid to thyself with
> the fear of the Lord upon thee, moved rather by the hope of be-

getting children than by any lust of thine. So, in the true line of
Abraham, thus shalt have joy of thy fatherhood.

(TOB. 6:22)

Instead then of reflecting in any way upon sex, the sacrament sees
generation as a reflection of the eternal generation of the Son in the bosom
of the Father. As St. Thomas Aquinas puts it: "If one is led to perform
the marriage act either by virtue of justice, in order to render the debt to
the partner, or by virtue of religion, that children may be procreated for
the worship of God, the act is meritorious."

As the sacrament sees in the father of the family the reflection of
Divine paternity, so there is in motherhood a relation to the Eucharist.
The mother says to her child, "As I live because of Christ, so you will live
because of me." As, under the species of bread, day by day Christ nourishes the Christian soul, so drop by drop the mother nourishes the child.
As the Divine Eucharist gives immortality, so this human eucharist of
motherhood is the guarantee of temporal life. The angel that once stood
at the gate of paradise to prevent man from eating the tree of life now
sheathes the sword. Life comes into its own. There is communion with
human life at the breast and Communion with divine life at the altar.

When the Son of God espoused humanity and became a Child, there
was a new emphasis on fecundity. It placed primacy at a point never
before seen in history. Up until the Incarnation, the order had been father,
mother, and child. Now it was turned backwards, and became child,
mother, and father. For centuries humans looked up to the heavens and
said: "God is away up there." But when a Mother held a Child in her
arms, it could truly be said that she looked *down* to Heaven. God was way
down there in the dust of human lives. If it be objected that Mary had
only one Child, it must be repeated that she had only one Child according
to the flesh, but she had other children according to the spirit, for Our
Blessed Lord said to her at the foot of the Cross: "Behold, thy son,"
referring to John. And John, being unnamed, stood for all humanity. At
that moment she became by divine decree the Mother of all whom Christ
redeemed and the Patroness of all mothers.

For Better or for Worse

Because of human frailty there may be, despite love's effort, a failure
to achieve common union in mind and body; but this does not give the
offended party the right to contract a new marriage. "What God, then, has
joined, let no man put asunder" (MATT. 19:6).

When human love and sex love break down, there is always Christian love, which steps in to suggest that the other person is to be regarded as a *gift* of God. Most of God's gifts are sweet; a few of them, however, are bitter. But whether bitter or sweet, the partner is still a gift of God, for whom the other must sacrifice himself or herself. Selfish love would seek to get rid of the burden of the other person simply because he is a burden. Christian love takes on the burden in obedience to the command: "Bear the burden of one another's failings; then you will be fulfilling the law of Christ" (GAL. 6:2).

What sickness is to an individual, an unhappy marriage may be to a couple; namely, a trial sent by God in order to perfect them spiritually. If a husband were suffering from pneumonia, the wife would not leave him. In like manner, if the husband is unfaithful or unkind, the wife will not leave him for another marriage. The acceptance of the trial of marriage is not a sentence to death. As a soldier is not sentenced to death because he takes an oath to his country, but admits that he is ready to face death rather than lose honor. Being wounded for the country we love is noble; being wounded for the God we love is nobler still.

Just as there is a communication of vital forces between husband and wife, so too, there can be a communication of spiritual forces: "The unbelieving husband has shared in his wife's consecration, and the unbelieving wife has shared in the consecration of one who is a brother" (I CORINTH. 7:14). What a blood transfusion is to the body, reparation for the sins of another is to the spirit. Instead of separating when there are trials, the Christian solution is to bear the cross for the sake of the sanctification of the other. A wife can redeem a husband, and a husband can redeem a wife, as Christ offered Himself for His spouse, the Church. As skin can be grafted from the back to the face, so merit can be applied from spouse to spouse. This spiritual communication may not have the romantic satisfaction in it of carnal communication, but its returns are eternal.

The great difference between a Christian and a pagan in such a trial is that the Christian *receives* suffering; he even speaks of it as coming from the hands of the Crucified; the unbeliever, however, finds no place for it in the universe because it negates his egotism; it cancels out his love of pleasure, and it begets an inferno within him. A cross to the Christian is outside him and therefore bearable; the double cross on the inside of the unbeliever is insoluble, unbearable.

Christian love not only can make such suffering bearable; it can even make it sweet. The Son of God voluntarily ended on a cross; but it did not conquer Him because it came from without: "He suffered under Pontius Pilate." The Christian, in like manner, sees that if Innocence did not spurn the cross, then somehow or other, it must fit into his life, which is far from innocent. Since marital love is the shadow cast on earth by the Love of Christ for His Church, then it must reflect Christ's redemptive quality. As Christ delivered Himself up for His spouse, so there will be some wives and some husbands who will deliver themselves up to Golgotha for the sake of their spouse.

Just as in the spiritual life there is the "dark night of the soul," so in marriage there is the dark night of the body. The ecstasy does not always endure. In the days of romance, the emphasis is on the ego's durability in love. Later on, the Christian sees that marriage is not two persons directed toward one another, but rather two going out to a common purpose beyond themselves.

When the Incarnate Son of God burst the bonds of death and rose to glory, Scripture revealed that the physical universe is groaning in pain until it is destined to be transformed as a perfect instrument of the spirit; that is, until there is a new heaven and a new earth. In the meantime, the Church makes use of the material things of this creation and associates action and prayer with it. Water, bread, wine, oil and other things are made the effectual signs of the spiritual gifts which God bestows upon His people through the Church as His agency. As Cardinal Newman put it:

> We approach and in spite of the darkness our hands, our head, our brow, or our lips become, as it were, sensible of the contact of something more than earthly. We know not where we are, but we have been bathing in water and a voice tells us that it is blood. Or we have a mark signed upon our forehead and it speaks of Calvary. Or we recollect a hand laid upon our heads and surely it had the print of the nails upon it and resembled Him Who gave sight to the blind and raised the dead. Or we have been eating or drinking, and it was not a dream surely that One fed us from His Wounded Side and renewed our nature by the heavenly meat He gave us.

It would be a false view to look on water, oil, bread, and the matter of sacraments as having any power of and by themselves. This was the mistake made by Naaman, the Syrian general, when Eliseus told him that he could be cured of his leprosy if he would bathe in the Jordan seven times. Naaman answered: "Has not Damascus its rivers, Abana and Phar-

140

phar, such water as is not to be found in Israel?" (IV KINGS 5:12). Thinking that the cure would be wrought through water alone, Naaman argued that the dirty water of the Jordan could not compare with the purer waters of his own land. Finally, at the urging of a servant, Naaman was healed and immediately saw that it was due to the power of God, not to the power of the waters. So it is in the sacraments. God uses men and matter; the power is not in them, but in God.

ABOUT THIS BOOK AND
THE MEN WHO MADE IT

FULTON JOHN SHEEN was born May 8, 1895, at El Paso, Illinois, one of four sons of Newton Morris and Delia (Fulton) Sheen. He was baptized Peter and took the name John at confirmation, later adopting his mother's maiden name. His father was a farmer, but the family later moved to Peoria, Illinois, where he attended St. Mary's School and Spalding Institute, from which he was graduated in 1913. He received his A.B. and M.A. degrees from St. Viator College, Bourbonnais, Illinois, where he first tasted the pleasures of speaking and writing as a member of the college debating team and newspaper staff. He completed his theological studies at St. Paul's Seminary, St. Paul, Minnesota, and was ordained to the priesthood for the Diocese of Peoria, September 20, 1919. A year later he obtained the degrees Bachelor of Sacred Theology and Bachelor of Canon Law from the Catholic University of America, and then went to the University of Louvain, Belgium, where he was awarded a Ph.D. in 1923. He also attended the Sorbonne in Paris and the Collegio Angelico in Rome. In 1924, he received his Doctorate of Sacred Theology in Rome and, a year later, while teaching dogmatic theology at St. Edmund's College, Ware, England, he was made an *Agrégé en Philosophie* by Louvain and awarded that university's Cardinal Mercier International Philosophy Award. Included among his honorary degrees are: LL.D., Litt.D., and L.H.D. On his return to the United States, he served as a curate at St. Patrick's Church in Peoria; joined the faculty of the Catholic University of America, Washington, D. C., in 1926 as a philosophy of religion instructor, and was later promoted to a full professorship. In June, 1934, he was appointed Papal Chamberlain and was elevated the following year to Domestic Prelate. He was consecrated Bishop on June 11, 1951, which was a year after he became National Director of the Society for the Propagation of the Faith. He has been heard by millions of people in the United States, Canada, and England through the media of radio and television. A prolific writer, he is author of two syndicated columns: "God Love You" for the Catholic Press, and "Bishop Sheen Speaks," for the secular press; and is editor of two magazines: *World-mission*, a quarterly review, and *Mission*, a bimonthly. The popularity of his radio and television programs can be judged from the fact that his daily mail, as a result of these programs, has reached as much as ten thousand letters in a single day—about one-third of them from non-Catholics. The largest single delivery of mail was thirty thousand letters. He conducted the first religious service ever telecast, served as narrator for a *March of Time* film, and has had his sermons issued in record album form. As well as serving in such organizations as the Catholic Literary Guild and the American Catholic Philosophical Society, he is an active member of the Mediaeval Academy and the American Geographical Association. The long list of his

142

Photo by Feliciano Garcia

Bishop Sheen officiates at the recent marriage of Yousuf and Estrellita (Nachbar) Karsh, Our Lady's Chapel, St. Patrick's Cathedral

books started with publication of *God and Intelligence in Modern Philosophy* (Longmans, Green, 1925). This was followed by *Religion Without God* (Longmans, Green, 1928), *The Life of All Living* (Century, 1930), *Old Errors and New Labels* (Century, 1931), *Moods and Truths* (Century, 1932), *The Way of the Cross* (Appleton-Century, 1934), *Seven Last Words* (Appleton-Century, 1933), *The Eternal Galilean* (Appleton-Century, 1934), *The Philosophy of Science* (Bruce, 1934), *The Mystical Body of Christ* (Sheed and Ward, 1935), *Calvary and the Mass* (Kenedy, 1936), *The Moral Universe* (Bruce, 1936), *The Cross and the Beatitudes* (Kenedy, 1937), *The Cross and the Crisis* (Bruce, 1938), *Liberty, Equality and Fraternity* (Macmillan, 1938), *The Rainbow of Sorrow* (Kenedy, 1938), *Victory Over Vice* (Kenedy, 1939), *Freedom Under God* (Bruce, 1940), *Whence Come Wars* (Sheed and Ward, 1940), *The Seven Virtues* (Kenedy, 1940), *For God and Country* (Kenedy, 1941), *A Declaration of Dependence* (Bruce, 1941), *God and War* (Kenedy, 1942), *The Divine Verdict* (Kenedy, 1943), *The Armor of God* (Kenedy, 1943), *Philosophies at War* (Scribner's, 1943), *Seven Words to the Cross* (Kenedy, 1944), *Seven Pillars of Peace*

(Scribner's, 1944), *Love One Another* (Kenedy, 1944), *Seven Words of Jesus and Mary* (Kenedy, 1945), *Preface to Religion* (Kenedy, 1946), *Characters of the Passion* (Kenedy, 1946), *Jesus, Son of Mary* (McMullen, 1947), *Communism and the Conscience of the West* (Bobbs, Merrill, 1948), *Philosophy of Religion* (Appleton-Century-Crofts, 1948), *Peace of Soul* (McGraw-Hill, 1949), *Lift Up Your Heart* (McGraw-Hill, 1950), *Three to Get Married* (Appleton-Century-Crofts, 1951), *The World's First Love* (McGraw-Hill, 1952), *Life Is Worth Living, First Series* (McGraw-Hill, 1953), *Life Is Worth Living, Second Series* (McGraw-Hill, 1954), *The Life of Christ* (McGraw-Hill, 1954), *The Way to Happiness* (Garden City, 1954), *Life Is Worth Living, Third Series* (McGraw-Hill, 1955), *The Way to Inner Peace* (Garden City, 1955), *God Love You* (Garden City, 1955), *Thinking Life Through* (Garden City, 1955), *The True Meaning of Christmas* (McGraw-Hill, 1955), *Life Is Worth Living, Fourth Series* (McGraw-Hill, 1956), *Thoughts for Daily Living* (Garden City, 1956), *Life Is Worth Living, Fifth Series* (McGraw-Hill, 1957), *This Is the Mass* (Hawthorn, 1958), *This Is Rome* (Hawthorn, 1960), *Go to Heaven* (McGraw-Hill, 1960), *This Is The Holy Land* (Hawthorn, 1961), and *The Fulton J. Sheen Sunday Missal* (Hawthorn, 1962). He is Auxiliary Bishop of New York.

YOUSUF KARSH was born on December 23, 1908, at Mardin, Armenia. He came to Canada at the age of fifteen during the Turkish massacres. Son of an import-export entrepreneur and grandson of an engraver, he went to stay with an uncle, A. G. Nakash, who owned a photography studio in Sherbrooke, Québec. He took an interest in the art of the camera and was sent by his uncle to Boston, Massachusetts, to study. After several years in the United States, he opened his own studio in Canada's capital where, within a few years, he was photographing the cream of society and leaders of government. When war broke out in 1939, Ottawa became a center of Allied war activity, and "Karsh of Ottawa" became a familiar signature on the portraits of some of the world's greatest leaders. In 1941, his famous portrait of Winston Churchill rocketed him to fame as the world's greatest portrait photographer. That photograph, along with seventy-four others which were taken in all parts of the world in the four years that followed, went into making his first book, *Faces of Destiny* (Ziff-Davis, 1946). He followed this with *This Is the Mass* (Hawthorn, 1958), *Portraits of Greatness* (Thomas Nelson & Sons, 1959), *This Is Rome* (Hawthorn, 1960), *This Is The Holy Land* (Hawthorn, 1961), and the publication of his memoirs in a work entitled *In Search of Greatness* (Knopf, 1962). Still a world traveler, he keeps cameras and equipment at studios in London, Paris, and New York, as well as in Ottawa. He usually carries a set of camera equipment that weighs at least 250 pounds. He always uses a white camera, finding that the traditional black is depressing, and his focusing cloth varies in color according to his own mood—though it is most often of red velvet with a gold satin lining. Groups of his portraits form part of the permanent collections of such museums as the Brooklyn Museum Department of Photography and the Museum of Modern Art in New York City; Eastman House, Rochester, New York; The Art Institute of Chicago; and the Huntington Library, San Marino, California. In acknowledgment of his contribution to Canadian art and culture, he received one of the first Canadian Citizenship Certificates in January, 1947, when Parliament passed a law creating Canadian citizenship.

A HAWTHORN BOOK